Romeo and Juliet: A Translation

Gabrielle Winters

Original Text by
William Shakespeare

Copyright © 2017 Gabrielle Winters
All rights reserved.
ISBN: 1-5209-0602-1
ISBN-13: 9781520906027

DEDICATION

For my siblings.
Who mean more to me than
they can possibly imagine.
Love you both.

ACKNOWLEDGMENTS

It goes without saying that I must undoubtedly (and obviously) acknowledge the great Mr Shakespeare for providing both the inspiration and basis for this work. The fact that his plays have survived over 400 years is a testament to their quality, worth, entertainment value and the everyman nature of their content.
I would also like to thank the friends and family who have supported me in this endeavour and never let me believe the naysayers who doubted my ability to pursue my dream of authorship.

NOTE FOR THE READER

To those who may be offended by my 'impertinence' in providing what I presumably believe to be a definitive translation of William Shakespeare's work, I would like to say that my intention is rather to provide an aid to those either seeking to better understand his text or who simply wish to approach his plays for the first time. My aim is to make Shakespeare more accessible to a wider audience and dismantle the barrier his archaic language can sometimes present to appreciating both the intricacies of his plots or the play on words and puns that course through the pages.

CONTENTS

Act I, Prologue	6
Act I, Scene I	8
Act I, Scene II	30
Act I, Scene III	40
Act I, Scene IV	50
Act I, Scene V	60
Act II, Prologue	74
Act II, Scene I	76
Act II, Scene II	80
Act II, Scene III	96
Act II, Scene IV	104
Act II, Scene V	124
Act II, Scene VI	130
Act III, Scene I	134
Act III, Scene II	150
Act III, Scene III	160
Act III, Scene IV	174
Act III, Scene V	178
Act IV, Scene I	198
Act IV, Scene II	208
Act IV, Scene III	214
Act IV, Scene IV	218
Act IV, Scene V	222
Act V, Scene I	234
Act V, Scene II	240
Act V, Scene III	244

ROMEO AND JULIET

ACT I

PROLOGUE
Two households, both alike in dignity,
In fair Verona, where we lay our scene,
From ancient grudge break to new mutiny,
Where civil blood makes civil hands unclean.
From forth the fatal loins of these two foes
A pair of star-cross'd lovers take their life;
Whose misadventured piteous overthrows
Do with their death bury their parents' strife.
The fearful passage of their death-mark'd love,
And the continuance of their parents' rage,
Which, but their children's end, nought could remove,
Is now the two hours' traffic of our stage;
The which if you with patient ears attend,
What here shall miss, our toil shall strive to mend.

ROMEO AND JULIET

ACT I

PROLOGUE
Two families of equal social standing
Live in Verona - where this play is set.
Their old feud causes new fighting,
And civilians end up fighting civilians.
From each of these two families,
Two unfortunate people take their own lives.
Their regrettable and tragic deaths
Bring an end to their families' fighting.
The sad story of their doomed romance
And their parents continuing dispute,
Which only their children's deaths could end,
Is what we'll show to you in the next two hours.
And, if you listen carefully,
What you missed here, you'll see in the play.

ACT I SCENE I. Verona. A public place.

Enter SAMPSON and GREGORY, of the house of Capulet, armed with swords and bucklers

SAMPSON
Gregory, on my word, we'll not carry coals.

GREGORY
No, for then we should be colliers.

SAMPSON
I mean, and we be in choler, we'll draw.

GREGORY
Ay, while you live, draw your neck out of collar.

SAMPSON
I strike quickly, being moved.

GREGORY
But thou art not quickly moved to strike.

SAMPSON
A dog of the house of Montague moves me.

GREGORY
To move is to stir; and to be valiant is to stand:
therefore, if thou art moved, thou runn'st away.

SAMPSON
A dog of that house shall move me to stand: I will
take the wall of any man or maid of Montague's.

GREGORY
That shows thee a weak slave, for the weakest goes
to the wall.

SAMPSON
'Tis true, and therefore women being the weaker vessels
are ever thrust to the wall: therefore I will push
Montague's men from the wall, and thrust his maids
to the wall.

ACT I SCENE I. Verona. A public place.

Enter SAMPSON and GREGORY, of the house of Capulet, armed with swords and bucklers

SAMPSON
Gregory, I swear to you, we're not made for hard labour.

GREGORY
No, because then we would be peasants.

SAMPSON
And, if we're treated as such, we'll retaliate.

GREGORY
Yes, if you're brave enough to risk your neck.

SAMPSON
I'm not afraid to act, when it's necessary.

GREGORY
But you don't often think it's necessary.

SAMPSON
Seeing one of the Montagues would make it necessary.

GREGORY
If it's necessary you draw and if you're brave you fight.
But, when it is necessary, you run away.

SAMPSON
Seeing one of the Montagues would make me stay. I'd
stand up against any man or woman that is a Montague.

GREGORY
That doesn't mean you're brave if all you'll do
is stand up.

SAMPSON
True - women, are believed to be weak,
And yet they stand up. So I will push
Montague's men out of the way, and push the women
up against the wall.

GREGORY
The quarrel is between our masters, and us their men.

SAMPSON
'Tis all one, I will show myself a tyrant: when I have fought with the men, I will be civil with the maids, I will cut off their heads.

GREGORY
The heads of the maids?

SAMPSON
Ay, the heads of the maids, or their maidenheads, take it in what sense thou wilt.

GREGORY
They must take it in sense that feel it.

SAMPSON
Me they shall feel while I am able to stand, and 'tis known I am a pretty piece of flesh.

GREGORY
'Tis well thou art not fish; if thou hadst, thou hadst been poor John. Draw thy tool, here comes of the house of the Montagues.

SAMPSON
My naked weapon is out. Quarrel, I will back thee.

GREGORY
How, turn thy back and run?

SAMPSON
Fear me not.

GREGORY
No, marry; I fear thee!

SAMPSON
Let us take the law of our sides, let them begin.

GREGORY
I will frown as I pass by, and let them take it as they list.

GREGORY
The fight is between our bosses and we're their servants.

SAMPSON
So it's the same thing. I will prove how great I am. When I have fought the men, I will deal with the
women and cut off their heads.

GREGORY
Cut off their heads?

SAMPSON
Yes, I will take their heads. Or take their virginity - whichever you like.

GREGORY
It's them that will have to like it.

SAMPSON
And they will like it for as long as I am able to stand. It's well known that I am a handsome man.

GREGORY
It's lucky you're not an animal. If you were, you'd be a pathetic creature. Draw your sword! Here come the Montagues.

SAMPSON
My sword is drawn. Start a fight – I'll back you up.

GREGORY
How? By turning and running away?

SAMPSON
Don't worry.

GREGORY
No, honestly - I worry!

SAMPSON
Let's get the law on our side and make them start it.

GREGORY
I will glare at them as I pass by, and they can take that how they want.

SAMPSON
Nay, as they dare. I will bite my thumb at them,
which is a disgrace to them, if they bear it.

Enter ABRAHAM and BALTHASAR

ABRAHAM
Do you bite your thumb at us, sir?

SAMPSON
I do bite my thumb, sir.

ABRAHAM
Do you bite your thumb at us, sir?

SAMPSON
[Aside to GREGORY] Is the law of our side if I say ay?

GREGORY
No.

SAMPSON
No, sir, I do not bite my thumb at you, sir, but I
bite my thumb, sir.

GREGORY
Do you quarrel, sir?

ABRAHAM
Quarrel, sir! No, sir.

SAMPSON
But if you do, sir, I am for you. I serve as good a man as you.

ABRAHAM
No better.

SAMPSON
Well, sir.

GREGORY
Say 'better', here comes one of my master's kinsmen.

SAMPSON
Yes, better, sir.

SAMPSON
Yes, if they dare. I will raise my finger at them,
which is an insult to them if they don't react.

Enter ABRAHAM and BALTHASAR

ABRAHAM
Did you raise your finger at us, sir?

SAMPSON
I did raise my finger, sir.

ABRAHAM
Did you raise your finger at us, sir?

SAMPSON
[Aside to GREGORY] Are we covered by the law, if I say yes?

GREGORY
No.

SAMPSON
No, sir, I didn't raise my finger at you, sir, but I
raised my finger , sir.

GREGORY
Do you have a problem, sir?

ABRAHAM
Problem sir? No, sir.

SAMPSON
If you do, sir, I'll take you on. My boss is as good as yours.

ABRAHAM
Not better?

SAMPSON
Well...

GREGORY
Say 'better' - here comes one of our boss's relatives.

SAMPSON
Yes, better, sir.

ABRAHAM
You lie.

SAMPSON
Draw, if you be men. Gregory, remember thy washing blow.

They fight

Enter BENVOLIO

BENVOLIO
Part, fools!
Put up your swords, you know not what you do.

Beats down their swords

Enter TYBALT

TYBALT
What, art thou drawn among these heartless hinds?
Turn thee, Benvolio, look upon thy death.

BENVOLIO
I do but keep the peace. Put up thy sword,
Or manage it to part these men with me.

TYBALT
What, drawn, and talk of peace! I hate the word,
As I hate hell, all Montagues, and thee:
Have at thee, coward.

They fight

Enter, several of both houses, who join the fray; then enter Citizens, with clubs

First Citizen
Clubs, bills, and partisans! Strike! Beat them down!
Down with the Capulets! Down with the Montagues!

Enter CAPULET in his gown, and LADY CAPULET

CAPULET
What noise is this? Give me my long sword, ho!

ABRAHAM
Liar.

SAMPSON
Fight, if you dare. Gregory, remember your killing blow.

They fight

Enter BENVOLIO

BENVOLIO
Stop, you idiots!
Put down your swords. Don't you see what you're doing?

Beats down their swords

Enter TYBALT

TYBALT
What are you doing with these young fools?
Turn around, Benvolio, and prepare to meet your doom.

BENVOLIO
I'm only trying to keep the peace. Put away your sword,
Or use it to help me stop them fighting.

TYBALT
Your sword drawn, and you talk of peace! I hate the word,
As much as I hate hell, all Montagues, and you.
Take this, you coward!

They fight

Enter, several of both houses, who join the fray; then enter Citizens, with clubs

First Citizen
Get out your weapons! Hit them! Beat them down!
Damn you, Capulets! Damn you, Montagues!

Enter CAPULET in his gown, and LADY CAPULET

CAPULET
What's all this noise? Give me my sword, quick!

LADY CAPULET
A crutch, a crutch! why call you for a sword?

CAPULET
My sword, I say! old Montague is come,
And flourishes his blade in spite of me.

Enter MONTAGUE and LADY MONTAGUE

MONTAGUE
Thou villain Capulet!--Hold me not, let me go.

LADY MONTAGUE
Thou shalt not stir a foot to seek a foe.

Enter PRINCE, with Attendants

PRINCE
Rebellious subjects, enemies to peace,
Profaners of this neighbour-stained steel,--
Will they not hear? - What, ho, you men, you beasts!
That quench the fire of your pernicious rage
With purple fountains issuing from your veins:
On pain of torture, from those bloody hands
Throw your mistemper'd weapons to the ground,
And hear the sentence of your moved prince.
Three civil brawls, bred of an airy word,
By thee, old Capulet, and Montague,
Have thrice disturbed the quiet of our streets,
And made Verona's ancient citizens
Cast by their grave beseeming ornaments
To wield old partisans, in hands as old,
Cankered with peace, to part your cankered hate:
If ever you disturb our streets again,
Your lives shall pay the forfeit of the peace.
For this time, all the rest depart away:
You Capulet; shall go along with me,
And, Montague, come you this afternoon,
To know our further pleasure in this case,
To old Free-town, our common judgment-place.
Once more, on pain of death, all men depart.

Exeunt all but MONTAGUE, LADY MONTAGUE, and BENVOLIO

LADY CAPULET
Rubbish! What do you need a sword for?

CAPULET
My sword. Now! Montague is here
And is waving his weapon to taunt me.

Enter MONTAGUE and LADY MONTAGUE

MONTAGUE
You evil man, Capulet. Don't hold me back, let me go.

LADY MONTAGUE
You mustn't do anything to cause trouble.

Enter PRINCE, with Attendants

PRINCE
All you disobedient people who are disturbing the peace,
And shamefully using their weapons on their neighbours.
Why won't they listen? Hey you! Men. You animals,
That only satisfy your destructive anger
When you draw blood from your opponents.
If you don't want to be tortured, from your bloody hands,
Throw your ill-used weapons to the ground
And listen to what I have to say.
Three public fights, caused by a pathetic grudge
Between you Capulet and Montague,
Have disturbed the peace in the town three times,
And made Verona's old citizens
Throw aside more suitable things
To wield old weapons, in hands that are just as old,
And rusty from lack of use to stop your ugly hate.
If you ever cause trouble in town again,
You shall pay for the disturbance with your lives.
For now, you can all go home.
Except you, Capulet - you come along with me.
And Montague - come back this afternoon
To know what else I have to say about this
To Freetown, where we hold our trials.
I'll say it once more, unless you want to die, leave now.

Exeunt all but MONTAGUE, LADY MONTAGUE, and BENVOLIO

MONTAGUE
Who set this ancient quarrel new abroach?
Speak, nephew, were you by when it began?

BENVOLIO
Here were the servants of your adversary,
And yours, close fighting ere I did approach:
I drew to part them: in the instant came
The fiery Tybalt, with his sword prepared,
Which, as he breathed defiance to my ears,
He swung about his head and cut the winds,
Who nothing hurt withal, hissed him in scorn:
While we were interchanging thrusts and blows,
Came more and more, and fought on part and part,
Till the prince came, who parted either part.

LADY MONTAGUE
O where is Romeo? saw you him to-day?
Right glad I am he was not at this fray.

BENVOLIO
Madam, an hour before the worshipped sun
Peered forth the golden window of the east,
A troubled mind drive me to walk abroad,
Where, underneath the grove of sycamore,
That westward rooteth from the city's side,
So early walking did I see your son;
Towards him I made, but he was ware of me,
And stole into the covert of the wood;
I, measuring his affections by my own,
Which then most sought where most might not be found,
Being one too many by my weary self,
Pursued my humour, not pursuing his,
And gladly shunned who gladly fled from me.

MONTAGUE
Many a morning hath he there been seen,
With tears augmenting the fresh morning dew,
Adding to clouds more clouds with his deep sighs,
But all so soon as the all-cheering sun
Should in the furthest east begin to draw
The shady curtains from Aurora's bed,
Away from the light steals home my heavy son,
And private in his chamber pens himself,
Shuts up his windows, locks far daylight out,
And makes himself an artificial night:

MONTAGUE
Who started all this up again?
Tell me, Benvolio, was it you who started it?

BENVOLIO
The servants of your enemy
And your own men were fighting fiercely when I arrived.
I drew my sword to stop them and at that point came
An angry Tybalt with his sword drawn
Which, as he said insulting things to me,
He swung around his head cutting the air,
But this didn't hurt anything – it just made a hissing noise.
While we were exchanging thrusts and blows,
More and more people came and fought each other
Until the Prince arrived and stopped it all.

LADY MONTAGUE
Where is Romeo? Have you seen him today?
I'm glad he wasn't involved in this.

BENVOLIO
Madam, an hour before the sun
Came over the horizon this morning,
I felt the need to go for a walk.
And underneath the grove of sycamore trees,
That grows in the west side of the city,
Although it was early, I saw your son out walking.
I moved towards him but he saw me
And dashed into the shelter of the wood.
I, judging his actions by what I would do
If I was found when I didn't want to be
And just wanted to be alone,
Decided to humour him by not pursuing him
And happily left alone the man who had left me.

MONTAGUE
He's been seen there many mornings,
His tears adding to the morning dew
And his sighs adding more air to the sky.
But as soon as the bright sun
Begins to rise in the east
And dawn begins to break,
He hurries home away from the sunlight
And hides himself in his room,
Shuts his windows, locks the daylight out
And makes himself an artificial night.

Black and portentous must this humour prove,
Unless good counsel may the cause remove.

BENVOLIO
My noble uncle, do you know the cause?

MONTAGUE
I neither know it, nor can learn of him.

BENVOLIO
Have you importuned him by any means?

MONTAGUE
Both by myself and many other friends:
But he, his own affections' counsellor,
Is to himself--I will not say how true—
But to himself so secret and so close,
So far from sounding and discovery,
As is the bud bit with an envious worm
Ere he can spread his sweet leaves to the air,
Or dedicate his beauty to the sun.
Could we but learn from whence his sorrows grow.
We would as willingly give cure as know.

Enter ROMEO

BENVOLIO
See, where he comes. So please you, step aside,
I'll know his grievance or be much denied.

MONTAGUE
I would thou wert so happy by thy stay,
To hear true shrift. Come, madam, let's away.

Exeunt MONTAGUE and LADY MONTAGUE

BENVOLIO
Good morrow, cousin.

ROMEO
Is the day so young?

BENVOLIO
But new struck nine.

It isn't good for him to be so gloomy.
We must find a way to help improve his mood.

BENVOLIO
Do you know why he's like this, uncle?

MONTAGUE
I don't know and he won't tell me.

BENVOLIO
Have you tried to get him to tell you?

MONTAGUE
Both by myself and through other friends.
But he prefers not to share
And keeps to himself - I don't know to what extent -
But to keep himself so secretive and withdrawn,
So far from being heard or seen,
Is as sad as when a flowerbud is bitten by a worm,
Before it can blossom into the air,
Or be allowed to show its beauty to the world.
If I only knew why he's like this,
I'd do all I could to help resolve it.

Enter ROMEO

BENVOLIO
Look, here he comes now. Please leave me with him -
I'll find out what's wrong if I possibly can.

MONTAGUE
I wish you had a happier reason to stay
Than to seek his confession. Come on, dear, let's go.

Exeunt MONTAGUE and LADY MONTAGUE

BENVOLIO
Hello, Romeo.

ROMEO
What time is it?

BENVOLIO
Only just gone nine.

ROMEO
Ay me, sad hours seem long.
Was that my father that went hence so fast?

BENVOLIO
It was. What sadness lengthens Romeo's hours?

ROMEO
Not having that, which, having, makes them short.

BENVOLIO
In love?

ROMEO
Out--

BENVOLIO
Of love?

ROMEO
Out of her favour where I am in love.

BENVOLIO
Alas that Love, so gentle in his view,
Should be so tyrannous and rough in proof!

ROMEO
Alas, that Love, whose view is muffled still,
Should, without eyes, see pathways to his will!
Where shall we dine? O me! What fray was here?
Yet tell me not, for I have heard it all:
Here's much to do with hate, but more with love:
Why then, O brawling love, O loving hate,
O any thing of nothing first create!
O heavy lightness, serious vanity,
Mis-shapen chaos of well-seeming forms,
Feather of lead, bright smoke, cold fire,
sick health,
Still-waking sleep, that is not what it is!
This love feel I, that feel no love in this.
Dost thou not laugh?

ROMEO
Goodness! Sadness makes the time drag.
Was that my father that just left so quickly?

BENVOLIO
It was. What' sadness is making the time drag?

ROMEO
Not having something that would make them go quicker.

BENVOLIO
Are you in love?

ROMEO
Out--

BENVOLIO
Of love?

ROMEO
Out of favour, with the woman I am in love with.

BENVOLIO
What a pity that love, that should be so kind,
Could be so cruel and mean in reality.

ROMEO
Yes. Love, that is known to be blind,
Can, even without eyes, find ways to do what it wants.
Where shall we eat? Oh goodness! What happened here?
No, don't tell me - I can probably guess.
It's a lot to do with hate, but also with family loyalty.
Why, then, should this troublesome love! Hated loyalty!
Something that has been caused by nothing important!
Such serious triviality! Violent pettiness!
Cause disorder in such well-mannered people!
It's like a feather of lead, bright smoke, cold fire,
sick health!
Being asleep but awake, yet that's not what it is!
The love I feel's like that, but I don't love feeling like that.
Don't you think that's funny?

BENVOLIO
No, coz, I rather weep.

ROMEO
Good heart, at what?

BENVOLIO
At thy good heart's oppression.

ROMEO
Why, such is love's transgression:
Griefs of mine own lie heavy in my breast,
Which thou wilt propagate, to have it pressed
With more of thine: this love that thou hast shown
Doth add more grief to too much of mine own.
Love is a smoke raised with the fume of sighs,
Being purged, a fire sparkling in lovers' eyes,
Being vexed a sea nourished with loving tears.
What is it else? a madness most discreet,
A choking gall, and a preserving sweet.
Farewell, my coz.

BENVOLIO
Soft, I will go along;
And if you leave me so, you do me wrong.

ROMEO
Tut, I have lost myself, I am not here,
This is not Romeo, he's some other where.

BENVOLIO
Tell me in sadness, who is that you love.

ROMEO
What, shall I groan and tell thee?

BENVOLIO
Groan? why, no;
But sadly tell me, who?

ROMEO
Bid a sick man in sadness make his will -
A word ill urged to one that is so ill:
In sadness, cousin, I do love a woman.

BENVOLIO
No, Romeo, I think it's sad.

ROMEO
Really, why?

BENVOLIO
That you're denied in love.

ROMEO
Ah, that's the way of love.
My sorrows make my heart heavy.
And you seem to be trying to add to it
With your own sorrows. The compassion you have shown
Makes my heart even heavier, it already weighs too much.
Love is undefined and made more so by uncertain things.
If requited, it causes a fire to sparkle in a lover's eyes.
If denied, it could fill a sea with all the tears that are shed.
What else is it? A hidden madness,
A suffocating problem and a sustaining delight.
Goodbye, Benvolio.

BENVOLIO
Wait! I will go with you.
If you leave me, I'll consider it an insult.

ROMEO
I don't feel like myself. Like I'm not here.
I'm not really Romeo, he's somewhere else.

BENVOLIO
Tell me seriously - who is it that you love?

ROMEO
What - should I groan and tell you?

BENVOLIO
Groan? No.
But, seriously, tell me who.

ROMEO
You might as well ask me to make my will.
If you force me to say the name that causes my grief.
Seriously, Benvolio, I am in love with a woman.

BENVOLIO
I aimed so near, when I supposed you loved.

ROMEO
A right good mark-man! and she's fair I love.

BENVOLIO
A right fair mark, fair coz, is soonest hit.

ROMEO
Well, in that hit you miss: she'll not be hit
With Cupid's arrow, she hath Dian's wit;
And in strong proof of chastity well armed,
From Love's weak childish bow she lives uncharmed.
She will not stay the siege of loving terms,
Nor bide th'encounter of assailing eyes,
Nor ope her lap to saint-seducing gold.
O, she is rich in beauty, only poor
That when she dies, with beauty dies her store.

BENVOLIO
Then she hath sworn that she will still live chaste?

ROMEO
She hath, and in that sparing makes huge waste:
For beauty starved with her severity
Cuts beauty off from all posterity.
She is too fair, too wise, wisely too fair,
To merit bliss by making me despair.
She hath forsworn to love, and in that vow
Do I live dead, that live to tell it now.

BENVOLIO
Be ruled by me, forget to think of her.

ROMEO
O teach me how I should forget to think.

BENVOLIO
By giving liberty unto thine eyes,
Examine other beauties.

BENVOLIO
I was right then when I said you were in love.

ROMEO
A very good guess! And the woman I love is beautiful.

BENVOLIO
A beautiful woman, Romeo, is easily won.

ROMEO
Well, by saying that you're wrong - she won't be won
By love. She has a razor sharp wit,
Is very protective of her chastity,
And won't be won over by childish attempts to woo her.
She won't listen to attempts at smooth talk,
And doesn't like people gazing at her lovingly,
And she won't give up her chastity for any amount of gold.
Her beauty is her only wealth - she is otherwise poor.
When she dies, her beauty dies with her.

BENVOLIO
Has she sworn that she will remain unmarried?

ROMEO
She has, and her doing so is such a waste
Because if she won't share her beauty
Then it will be lost forever.
She is too pretty, too clever, and also not the type
To seek amusement in making me unhappy.
She has promised not to fall in love and, in doing so,
Has effectively killed the man who's now telling you this.

BENVOLIO
Listen to me - forget about her.

ROMEO
And just how do I do that?

BENVOLIO
By allowing yourself to look around
And see other beautiful women.

ROMEO
'Tis the way
To call hers exquisite, in question more:
These happy masks that kiss fair ladies' brows,
Being black, put us in mind they hide the fair;
He that is strucken blind cannot forget
The precious treasure of his eyesight lost;
Show me a mistress that is passing fair,
What doth her beauty serve but as a note
Where I may read who passed that passing fair?
Farewell, thou canst not teach me to forget.

BENVOLIO
I'll pay that doctrine, or else die in debt.

Exeunt

ROMEO
By doing this,
I'll only think her more beautiful.
The pleasant expressions that beautiful ladies' wear
are false. But make us think they must be beautiful.
A man who is struck blind doesn't forget
How much he liked being able to see.
Show me a woman who is fairly beautiful.
What use is her beauty except to
Enable me to see who else notices her?
Goodbye. You can't make me forget.

BENVOLIO
I'll prove I can, if it's the last thing I do.

Exeunt

ACT I SCENE II. A street.

Enter CAPULET, PARIS, and Servant

CAPULET
But Montague is bound as well as I,
In penalty alike, and 'tis not hard, I think,
For men so old as we to keep the peace.

PARIS
Of honourable reckoning are you both,
And pity 'tis, you lived at odds so long.
But now, my lord, what say you to my suit?

CAPULET
But saying o'er what I have said before:
My child is yet a stranger in the world,
She hath not seen the change of fourteen years;
Let two more summers wither in their pride,
Ere we may think her ripe to be a bride.

PARIS
Younger than she are happy mothers made.

CAPULET
And too soon marred are those so early made.
The earth hath swallowed all my hopes but she;
She is the hopeful lady of my earth.
But woo her, gentle Paris, get her heart,
My will to her consent is but a part;
And she agreed, within her scope of choice
Lies my consent and fair according voice.
This night I hold an old accustomed feast,
Whereto I have invited many a guest,
Such as I love, and you, among the store,
One more, most welcome, makes my number more.
At my poor house look to behold this night
Earth-treading stars that make dark heaven light.
Such comfort as do lusty young men feel
When well-apparelled April on the heel
Of limping winter treads, even such delight

ACT I SCENE II. A street.

Enter CAPULET, PARIS, and Servant

CAPULET
But Montague is in the same position as me -
We face the same punishment. And it shouldn't be hard
For men as old as us to keep the peace.

PARIS
You're both very honourable men.
And it's a pity you've been fighting for so long.
But now, sir, what do you say to my proposal?

CAPULET
Nothing different to what I have said before.
My daughter is still very young -
She is not yet fourteen years old.
In two more years from now
She might be old enough to be married.

PARIS
Women younger than her have had children.

CAPULET
Yes, and they're scarred from doing so that young.
She is all I have left to live for
And represents all my hopes for the future.
But you could woo her, Paris, and win her heart -
You don't just need my consent.
If she agrees and chooses you
Then I will give you my consent and my blessing.
Tonight I am having a banquet,
To which I have invited many people
That I like. And you could come too -
One more person would be very welcome at the party.
At my house tonight you will see
Many important people that brighten our lives.
It will be as enjoyable as it is for young people
When the bright spring arrives to banish
The miserable winter. Happiness such as this

Among fresh fennel buds shall you this night
Inherit at my house; hear all, all see;
And like her most whose merit most shall be;
Which on more view of many, mine, being one
May stand in number, though in reck'ning none,
Come go with me.

To Servant, giving a paper

Go, sirrah, trudge about
Through fair Verona, find those persons out
Whose names are written there, and to them say,
My house and welcome on their pleasure stay.

Exeunt CAPULET and PARIS

Servant
Find them out whose names are written here! It is
written that the shoemaker should meddle with his
yard and the tailor with his last, the fisher with
his pencil, and the painter with his nets; but I am
sent to find those persons whose names are here
writ, and can never find what names the writing
person hath here writ. I must to the learned. In good time!

Enter BENVOLIO and ROMEO

BENVOLIO
Tut, man, one fire burns out another's burning,
One pain is lessened by another's anguish;
Turn giddy, and be holp by backward turning;
One desperate grief cures with another's languish:
Take thou some new infection to thy eye,
And the rank poison of the old will die.

ROMEO
Your plaintain leaf is excellent for that.

BENVOLIO
For what, I pray thee?

Among many pretty young women, you will tonight
Experience at my house. Listen and look carefully
And love the one who most deserves your affection.
Even though she'll be one of many,
When compared with others, there's none like her.
Come with me.

To Servant, giving a paper

You - go throughout
The town and find the people
Whose names are on this list. Tell them,
I look forward to seeing them at my house.

Exeunt CAPULET and PARIS

Servant
Find the people on this list! It is
possible that a shoemaker could use a tailor's
ruler and a tailor the shoemaker's tool. An angler could
use a painter's pencil and a painter an angler's nets. But I
have been sent to find the people whose names are on
this list, but I don't know what names are on
this list. I must find someone who can read. And quick.

Enter BENVOLIO and ROMEO

BENVOLIO
Oh, come on. Someone's problem will outweigh another's.
Someone's worries will seem less compared to another's.
Turn that around and you'll see what I mean.
One person's troubles can help soothe another's distress.
If you find something else to focus on,
You'll soon forget what you're currently obsessed with.

ROMEO
Your advice is very good.

BENVOLIO
For what?

ROMEO
For your broken shin.

BENVOLIO
Why, Romeo, art thou mad?

ROMEO
Not mad, but bound more than a madman is:
Shut up in prison, kept without my food,
Whipt and tormented, and--God-den, good fellow.

Servant
God gi' god-den. I pray, sir, can you read?

ROMEO
Ay, mine own fortune in my misery.

Servant
Perhaps you have learned it without book; but I
pray, can you read any thing you see?

ROMEO
Ay, if I know the letters and the language.

Servant
Ye say honestly, rest you merry.

ROMEO
Stay, fellow, I can read.

Reads

'Signior Martino and his wife and daughters,
County Anselme and his beauteous sisters, the lady
widow of Vitravio, Signior Placentio and his lovely
nieces, Mercutio and his brother Valentine, mine
uncle Capulet, his wife and daughters, my fair niece
Rosaline, and Livia, Signior Valentio and his cousin
Tybalt, Lucio and the lively Helena.' A fair
assembly: whither should they come?

ROMEO
For helping you.

BENVOLIO
Why are you angry, Romeo?

ROMEO
I'm not, but I feel I'm being punished as if I had been.
I'm imprisoned by my love, kept from what I want,
Which is torture and... Hello there.

Servant
Good evening. Please, sir, can you read?

ROMEO
Yes - one thing to be positive about in my misery.

Servant
Maybe you got that without reading. But,
anyway, can you read anything you are given?

ROMEO
Yes, if it's in a language I know.

Servant
That's very honest of you. Goodbye.

ROMEO
Wait. I said I can read.

Reads

Mr Martino and his wife and daughters,
Count Anselme and his beautiful sisters,
Vitravio's widow, Mr Placentio and his
lovely nieces, Mercutio and his brother, Valentine, my
uncle Capulet, his wife and daughters, my niece,
Rosaline, Livia, Mr Valentio and his cousin,
Tybalt, Lucio and the wonderful Helena.' That's a nice
bunch of people. Where are they going?

Servant
Up.

ROMEO
Whither? To supper?

Servant
To our house.

ROMEO
Whose house?

Servant
My master's.

ROMEO
Indeed I should have asked you that before.

Servant
Now I'll tell you without asking. My master is the
great rich Capulet, and if you be not of the house
of Montagues, I pray come and crush a cup of wine.
Rest you merry.

Exit

BENVOLIO
At this same ancient feast of Capulet's
Sups the fair Rosaline whom thou so loves,
With all the admired beauties of Verona:
Go thither, and, with unattainted eye
Compare her face with some that I shall show,
And I will make thee think thy swan a crow.

ROMEO
When the devout religion of mine eye
Maintains such falsehood, then turn tears to fires;
And these who, often drowned, could never die,
Transparent heretics, be burnt for liars.
One fairer than my love! the all-seeing sun
Ne'er saw her match since first the world begun.

Servant
Up.

ROMEO
Where? To dinner?

Servant
To our house.

ROMEO
Whose house?

Servant
My boss's.

ROMEO
Ah, I should have asked you that first.

Servant
And I'll tell you now without asking - my boss is the
Very rich Capulet. And, if you are not one of the
Montagues, you're welcome to come have a glass of wine.
Goodbye!

Exit

BENVOLIO
At this banquet of Capulet's
Will be Rosaline who you are in love with,
Along with all the other pretty women of Verona.
Go there and, with an unbiased eye,
Compare her face to another that I'll point out to you
And you'll realise she's not as pretty as you thought.

ROMEO
If my own eyes
Ever made me believe that rubbish, I'd be very angry.
Even though I never thought they'd mislead me,
They will have betrayed me and I won't trust them again!
Someone prettier than Rosaline? There has
Never been another like her since history began.

BENVOLIO
Tut, you saw her fair, none else being by,
Herself poised with herself in either eye;
But in that crystal scales let there be weighed
Your lady's love against some other maid
That I will show you shining at this feast,
And she shall scant show well that now shows best.

ROMEO
I'll go along no such sight to be shown,
But to rejoice in splendour of mine own.

Exeunt

BENVOLIO
But you only thought her pretty as no-one else was around.
She was the only one you could see.
But now you'll have the chance to compare
Her beauty against another's
That I will point out to you at the banquet.
And what seems pretty now won't seem so then.

ROMEO
I'll go, not because I think you're right,
But to enjoy seeing Rosaline again.

Exeunt

ACT I SCENE III. A room in Capulet's house.

Enter LADY CAPULET and Nurse

LADY CAPULET
Nurse, where's my daughter? call her forth to me.

NURSE
Now, by my maidenhead, at twelve year old,
I bade her come. What, lamb! What, ladybird!
God forbid, where's this girl? What, Juliet!

Enter JULIET

JULIET
How now, who calls?

NURSE
Your mother.

JULIET
Madam, I am here,
what is your will?

LADY CAPULET
This is the matter. Nurse, give leave a while,
We must talk in secret. Nurse, come back again,
I have remembered me, thou s' hear our counsel.
Thou knowest my daughter's of a pretty age.

NURSE
Faith, I can tell her age unto an hour.

LADY CAPULET
She's not fourteen.

NURSE
I'll lay fourteen of my teeth,--
And yet, to my teen be it spoken, I have but four--
She is not fourteen. How long is it now
To Lammas-tide?

LADY CAPULET
A fortnight and odd days.

ACT I SCENE III. A room in Capulet's house.

Enter LADY CAPULET and Nurse

LADY CAPULET
Nurse, where's my daughter? Tell her to come here.

NURSE
I swear, on my honour (when I was twelve),
I told her to come. Darling! Sweetheart!
Goodness me! Where is that girl? Oh, Juliet!

Enter JULIET

JULIET
Yes! Who wants me?

NURSE
Your mother.

JULIET
Mum, I'm here.
What do you want?

LADY CAPULET
I'll tell you… Nurse, leave us alone for a while -
We need to talk in secret. Nurse, come back again.
I've remembered I decided you needed to hear this too.
You know my daughter is young.

NURSE
Yes, I can tell how old she is to within the hour.

LADY CAPULET
She's not yet fourteen.

NURSE
Yes, I'll bet my teeth on it. -
Although, having said that, I only have four -
She is not yet fourteen. How long is it now
Until August?

LADY CAPULET
Just over a fortnight.

NURSE
Even or odd, of all days in the year,
Come Lammas-eve at night shall she be fourteen.
Susan and she - God rest all Christian souls!--
Were of an age. Well, Susan is with God,
She was too good for me. But as I said,
On Lammas-eve at night shall she be fourteen,
That shall she, marry, I remember it well.
'Tis since the earthquake now eleven years,
And she was weaned - I never shall forget it -
Of all the days of the year, upon that day;
For I had then laid wormwood to my dug,
Sitting in the sun under the dove-house wall.
My lord and you were then at Mantua -
Nay, I do bear a brain - but as I said,
When it did taste the wormwood on the nipple
Of my dug and felt it bitter, pretty fool,
To see it tetchy and fall out wi'th dug!
'Shake!' quoth the dove-house; 'twas no need, I trow,
To bid me trudge.
And since that time it is eleven years,
For then she could stand high-lone; nay, by th'rood,
She could have run and waddled all about;
For even the day before, she broke her brow,
And then my husband- God be with his soul,
'A was a merry man - took up the child.
'Yea', quoth he, 'dost thou fall upon thy face?
Thou wilt fall backward when thou hast more wit,
Wilt thou not, Jule?' And, by my holidam,
The pretty wretch left crying, and said 'Ay'.
To see now how a jest shall come about!
I warrant, and I should live a thousand years,
I never should forget it: 'Wilt thou not, Jule?" quoth he,
And, pretty fool, it stinted, and said 'Ay'.

LADY CAPULET
Enough of this, I pray thee hold thy peace.

NURSE
Over or under, it doesn't matter,
On 31st August she'll be fourteen.
She and my daughter, Susan - may she rest in peace -
Were the same age. But Susan is with God.
She was too good for this earth. But, as I said,
On 31st August she'll be fourteen.
Yes, she will. I remember it well.
It's eleven years since the earthquake.
And she was weaned - I shall never forget it -
Of all days, on that day.
I had just prepared to feed her
While sitting in the sun under the dovecote -
You and your husband were in Mantua -
No, I know I'm right! But, as I was saying,
When she tasted the bitter stuff I'd put on the nipple
Of my breast and thought it unpleasant, poor thing,
She got tetchy and refused to suckle!
The dovecote shook and there was no need, I can tell you,
To tell me to move.
Since then it's been eleven years.
And she could stand on her own then. No, I swear,
She could have run and waddled all around.
But just the day before she hit her head
And my husband - God rest his soul -
He was a merry man - picked her up.
'What?' he said, 'Did you fall on your face?
You'll fall backwards when you've got more sense.
Won't you, Jules?' And, I swear,
The little thing stopped crying and said, 'Yes.'
You see how funny that was?
I swear, if I should live a thousand years,
I will never forget it. 'Won't you, Jules?' he said.
And she, little thing, stopped crying and said 'Yes.'

LADY CAPULET
Enough. Please, be quiet.

NURSE
Yes, madam, yet I cannot choose but laugh,
To think it should leave crying, and say 'Ay':
And yet I warrant it had upon its brow
A bump as big as a young cock'rel's stone,
A perilous knock, and it cried bitterly.
'Yea', quoth my husband, 'fall'st upon thy face?
Thou wilt fall backward when thou comest to age,
Wilt thou not, Jule?' It stinted, and said 'Ay'.

JULIET
And stint thou too, I pray thee, Nurse, say I.

NURSE
Peace, I have done. God mark thee to his grace,
Thou wast the prettiest babe that e'er I nursed.
And I might live to see thee married once,
I have my wish.

LADY CAPULET
Marry, that 'marry' is the very theme
I came to talk of. Tell me, daughter Juliet,
How stands your dispositions to be married?

JULIET
It is an honour that I dream not of.

NURSE
An honour! were not I thine only nurse,
I would say thou hadst suck'd wisdom from thy teat.

LADY CAPULET
Well, think of marriage now; younger than you,
Here in Verona, ladies of esteem,
Are made already mothers. By my count,
I was your mother much upon these years
That you are now a maid. Thus then in brief:
The valiant Paris seeks you for his love.

NURSE
Yes, madam. But I can't help but laugh -
To think she should stop crying and say 'Yes.'
And yet, I swear, that on her head there was
A bump as big as a cockerel's ball.
A nasty knock. And she cried a lot.
'What?' said my husband, 'You fell on your face?
You'll fall backwards when you're older.
Won't you, Jules?' She stopped and said 'Yes.'

JULIET
And you can stop too. Please, nurse, I insist.

NURSE
Alright, I've finished. But God knows
You were the prettiest baby that I ever cared for.
And I hope I live to see you married one day.
That would be my wish.

LADY CAPULET
Yes, marriage is exactly what
I came to talk about. Tell me, Juliet,
How do you feel about getting married?

JULIET
It would be an honour but I don't really think about it.

NURSE
Well said! If it weren't for the fact I'm your nurse,
I'd say you'd sucked wisdom from my breast.

LADY CAPULET
Well, think about it now. Women younger than you,
Here in Verona - ladies of noble birth -
Have already become mothers. I mean,
I was your mother when I was a similar age
To what you are now. Anyway, in short,
Paris seeks your hand in marriage.

NURSE
A man, young lady! lady, such a man
As all the world - Why, he's a man of wax.

LADY CAPULET
Verona's summer hath not such a flower.

NURSE
Nay, he's a flower, in faith, a very flower.

LADY CAPULET
What say you, can you love the gentleman?
This night you shall behold him at our feast;
Read o'er the volume of young Paris' face,
And find delight writ there with beauty's pen;
Examine every married lineament,
And see how one another lends content;
And what obscured in this fair volume lies
Find written in the margent of his eyes.
This precious book of love, this unbound lover,
To beautify him, only lacks a cover.
The fish lives in the sea, and 'tis much pride
For fair without the fair within to hide;
That book in many's eyes doth share the glory
That in gold clasps locks in the golden story:
So shall you share all that he doth possess,
By having him, making yourself no less.

NURSE
No less! nay, bigger women grow by men.

LADY CAPULET
Speak briefly, can you like of Paris' love?

JULIET
I'll look to like, if looking liking move;
But no more deep will I endart mine eye
Than your consent gives strength to make it fly.

NURSE
He's a good man, my dear. And what a man!
The best in all the world - he's so perfect.

LADY CAPULET
There's not another like him in Verona.

NURSE
No, he's one of a kind. Truly, one of a kind.

LADY CAPULET
What do you think? Could you love him?
You'll see him tonight at our banquet.
Take a good look at his face
And you'll see he's a very handsome man.
Examine every single detail
And notice how they compliment each other
And what you can't see in his face
You can see in his eyes.
This special suitor, this single man,
Just needs one more thing to complete him.
He's been waiting for you. And it's not unreasonable
To think that there's more to him than we can see.
Many people can see how wonderful he is
But there might be more about him hidden away.
And you'll share everything he has.
By marrying him, you won't be any worse off for it.

NURSE
Not at all! He'll make you seem even better.

LADY CAPULET
Tell me quickly - could you like Paris?

JULIET
I'll look at him and see if I like him.
But I won't do any more than that
Unless you're happy for me to do so.

Enter a Servant

Servant
Madam, the guests are come, supper served up, you called, my young lady asked for, the Nurse cursed in the pantry, and every thing in extremity. I must hence to wait, I beseech you follow straight.

LADY CAPULET
We follow thee.

Exit Servant

Juliet, the County stays.

NURSE
Go, girl, seek happy nights to happy days.

Exeunt

Enter a Servant

Servant
Madam, the guests have arrived, dinner is served, you have
been called for, Juliet too, the nurse is needed in
the pantry, and everything is working flat out. I must
go back now. But I beg you to come soon.

LADY CAPULET
We'll come now.

Exit Servant

Juliet, Paris is waiting for you.

NURSE
Go on, Juliet. I hope you'll be very happy.

Exeunt

ACT I SCENE IV. A street.

Enter ROMEO, MERCUTIO, BENVOLIO, with five or six Maskers, Torch-bearers, and others

ROMEO
What, shall this speech be spoke for our excuse?
Or shall we on without apology?

BENVOLIO
The date is out of such prolixity:
We'll have no Cupid hoodwinked with a scarf,
Bearing a Tartar's painted bow of lath,
Scaring the ladies like a crow-keeper,
Nor no without-book prologue, faintly spoke
After the prompter, for our entrance;
But let them measure us by what they will,
We'll measure them a measure and be gone.

ROMEO
Give me a torch, I am not for this ambling;
Being but heavy, I will bear the light.

MERCUTIO
Nay, gentle Romeo, we must have you dance.

ROMEO
Not I, believe me. You have dancing shoes
With nimble soles, I have a soul of lead
So stakes me to the ground I cannot move.

MERCUTIO
You are a lover, borrow Cupid's wings,
And soar with them above a common bound.

ROMEO
I am too sore enpierced with his shaft
To soar with his light feathers, and so bound
I cannot bound a pitch above dull woe:
Under love's heavy burden do I sink.

MERCUTIO
And to sink in it should you burden love,
Too great oppression for a tender thing.

ACT I SCENE IV. A street.

Enter ROMEO, MERCUTIO, BENVOLIO, with five or six Maskers, Torch-bearers, and others

ROMEO
What shall we say to excuse ourselves if we're caught?
Or shall we carry on regardless?

BENVOLIO
It's too late to worry about that.
We won't let our plans be ruined with such worries.
We're on the hunt for women.
We'll make them jump like a scarecrow does birds
And no improvised introduction, whispered
To the herald at the door, will announce our arrival.
Let them think of us what they want -
We're more than a match for them - then we'll be gone.

ROMEO
Give me a torch. I'm not in the mood for this.
As I feel so heavy-hearted, I'll carry the light.

MERCUTIO
No, Romeo, you must join in the dancing.

ROMEO
No, not me, honestly. You want to dance
And are feeling light-hearted. I have a heavy heart
And it weighs me down so much I cannot move.

MERCUTIO
You are in love so let love lift you
And fly away from all your cares.

ROMEO
I'm still too sore from the effects of love
To fly away from my cares. And, feeling like this,
I cannot be anything other than miserable.
The weight of the sadness caused by love holds me down.

MERCUTIO
And, if you let it, you'll be letting it down.
Because such weight is too great for such a fragile thing.

ROMEO
Is love a tender thing? it is too rough,
Too rude, too boist'rous, and it pricks like thorn.

MERCUTIO
If love be rough with you, be rough with love:
Prick love for pricking, and you beat love down.
Give me a case to put my visage in,
A visor for a visor! what care I
What curious eye doth quote deformities?
Here are the beetle brows shall blush for me.

BENVOLIO
Come knock and enter, and no sooner in,
But every man betake him to his legs.

ROMEO
A torch for me: let wantons light of heart
Tickle the senseless rushes with their heels;
For I am proverb'd with a grandsire phrase,
I'll be a candle-holder, and look on:
The game was ne'er so fair, and I am done.

MERCUTIO
Tut, dun's the mouse, the constable's own word.
If thou art Dun, we'll draw thee from the mire,
Or save your reverence love, wherein thou stickest
Up to the ears. Come, we burn daylight, ho!

ROMEO
Nay, that's not so.

MERCUTIO
I mean, sir, in delay
We waste our lights in vain, like lamps by day.
Take our good meaning, for our judgment sits
Five times in that ere once in our five wits.

ROMEO
And we mean well in going to this mask,
But 'tis no wit to go.

MERCUTIO
Why, may one ask?

ROMEO
Is love fragile? I think it's rough,
Unpleasant, vicious, and it hurts like a knife.

MERCUTIO
If love is hard on you, be hard on love.
Discard love for hurting you and shake off its effects.
Give me a mask for my face.
A mask for someone who's hiding! I won't care
If anyone notices that I'm there
This is the face that that they will see.

BENVOLIO
Come on, let's knock and go in. And, once we're in,
Be prepared to run.

ROMEO
I'll carry the torch. Those who are light-hearted
Can enjoy the dancing
But I can't shake off how I feel.
So I'll carry the torch and watch.
Dancing doesn't interest me - I'm done.

MERCUTIO
No, mice are dun-coloured - ask anyone.
If you are dun, I'll soon draw you out of this mud -
Oh, forgive me, you call it love - which you're stuck in
Up to your ears. Come on, we're wasting time. Let's go!

ROMEO
No, we're not.

MERCUTIO
But Romeo by delaying
We waste our torches as we would sunlight in the daytime.
You know what I mean. And what I say is
Five times as true because there are five of us.

ROMEO
We don't mean any harm by going to the banquet.
But that still doesn't mean we should go.

MERCUTIO
Why not, may I ask?

ROMEO
I dreamt a dream tonight.

MERCUTIO
And so did I.

ROMEO
Well, what was yours?

MERCUTIO
That dreamers often lie.

ROMEO
In bed asleep, while they do dream things true.

MERCUTIO
O then I see Queen Mab hath been with you:
She is the fairies' midwife, and she comes
In shape no bigger than an agate-stone
On the forefinger of an alderman,
Drawn with a team of little atomi
Over men's noses as they lie asleep.
Her chariot is an empty hazel-nut,
Made by the joiner squirrel or old grub,
Time out a'mind the fairies' coachmakers:
Her waggon-spokes made of long spinners' legs,
The cover of the wings of grasshoppers,
The traces of the smallest spider web,
The collars of the moonshine's wat'ry beams,
Her whip of cricket's bone, the lash of film,
Her waggoner a small grey-coated gnat,
Not half so big as a round little worm
Pricked from the lazy finger of a maid.
And in this state she gallops night by night
Through lovers' brains, and then they dream of love,
O'er courtiers' knees, that dream on cur'sies straight,
O'er lawyers' fingers, who straight dream on fees,
O'er ladies' lips, who straight on kisses dream,
Which oft the angry Mab with blisters plagues,
Because their breaths with sweetmeats tainted are.
Sometime she gallops o'er a courtier's nose,
And then dreams he of smelling out a suit;

ROMEO
I had a dream last night.

MERCUTIO
And so did I.

ROMEO
Well, what did you dream?

MERCUTIO
That dreams don't tell the truth.

ROMEO
But while asleep, you might dream of things that are true.

MERCUTIO
You're making a lot of fuss over a dream.
It must have been caused by the fairy Mab, who is
No bigger than a gemstone
Worn in the ring on the forefinger of a nobleman,
Drawn by a group of tiny specks,
Over men's noses while they sleep.
Her coach is an empty hazelnut shell
Made by a squirrel or old worms,
Who have always made coaches for fairies.
Her wheel spokes are made of spiders' legs,
The roof of grasshoppers' wings,
The windows of the thinnest spider's web,
The reins of moonbeams,
Her whip handle of cricket bone, and the lash of gauze.
Her coachman is a small grey gnat,
Not half as big as a little worm
Found on the finger of a girl.
And this is how she travels night after night
Through lovers' minds and then they dream of love.
Over courtiers' knees, so they dream of dutiful courtesies.
Over lawyers' fingers, who then dream about fees.
Over ladies ' lips, who then dream about kisses,
Which the fairy will often plague with blisters
Because their breath stinks of sweets.
Sometimes she goes over a courtier's nose
And then he dreams of finding a profit

And sometime comes she with a tithe-pig's tail
Tickling a parson's nose as 'a lies asleep,
Then he dreams of another benefice.
Sometime she driveth o'er a soldier's neck,
And then dreams he of cutting foreign throats,
Of breaches, ambuscadoes, Spanish blades,
Of healths five-fathom deep; and then anon
Drums in his ear, at which he starts and wakes,
And being thus frighted, swears a prayer or two,
And sleeps again. This is that very Mab
That plats the manes of horses in the night,
And bakes the elf-locks in foul sluttish hairs,
Which, once untangled, much misfortune bodes.
This is the hag, when maids lie on their backs,
That presses them and learns them first to bear,
Making them women of good carriage.
This is she -

ROMEO
Peace, peace, Mercutio, peace!
Thou talk'st of nothing.

MERCUTIO
True, I talk of dreams,
Which are the children of an idle brain,
Begot of nothing but vain fantasy,
Which is as thin of substance as the air,
And more inconstant than the wind, who woos
Even now the frozen bosom of the north,
And, being angered, puffs away from thence,
Turning his side to the dew-dropping south.

BENVOLIO
This wind you talk of blows us from ourselves:
Supper is done, and we shall come too late.

And sometime she comes with the hint of a trail,
Tickling a parson's nose as he lies asleep,
Then he dreams of getting another benefactor.
Sometimes she goes over a soldier's neck
And then dreams he of cutting enemy throats -
Of battles, ambushes, sharp swords,
Of lots of drink. And then he hears
Drumming in his ear at which point he jolts and wakes up
And, being frightened, says a prayer or two
And then falls asleep again. This is the same fairy
That plaits the manes of horses at night
Putting knots in unkempt hair,
Which, when undone, are believed to bring misfortune.
This is the witch who, when girls lie on their backs,
Visits them and makes them reach maturity
So they will soon be able to bear children.
This is the…

ROMEO
Be quiet, Mercutio. Quiet!
This is all meaningless.

MERCUTIO
True - I'm talking about dreams,
Which are the product of an idle mind,
Created from nothing but fantasy,
Which is as insubstantial as air
And more unpredictable than wind, that blows
Even now in the cold reaches of the north,
Until it's all worked up and blows away from there
Towards the humid south.

BENVOLIO
All this talk of wind is distracting us from our own course.
Dinner will be over and we will be too late.

ROMEO
I fear too early, for my mind misgives
Some consequence yet hanging in the stars
Shall bitterly begin his fearful date
With this night's revels, and expire the term
Of a despisèd life closed in my breast,
By some vile forfeit of untimely death.
But He that hath the steerage of my course
Direct my sail! On, lusty gentlemen.

BENVOLIO
Strike, drum.

Exeunt

ROMEO
I think we'll be too early. I've got a bad feeling
That some unknown destiny that is waiting to happen
Will start to come true tonight
At the party and lead to the end
Of the life that beats in my chest
By something that will cause my untimely death.
But God will guide me through my life
And keep me on the right path! Let's go.

BENVOLIO
Onwards.

Exeunt

ACT I SCENE V. A hall in Capulet's house.

Musicians waiting. Enter Servingmen with napkins

First Servant
Where's Potpan, that he helps not to take away? He shift a trencher? he scrape a trencher!

Second Servant
When good manners shall lie all in one or two men's hands, and they unwashed too, 'tis a foul thing.

First Servant
Away with the join-stools, remove the court-cupboard, look to the plate. Good thou, save me a piece of marchpane, and, as thou loves me, let the porter let in Susan Grindstone and Nell. Antony and Potpan!

Second Servant
Ay, boy, ready.

First Servant
You are looked for and called for, asked for and sought for, in the great chamber.

Second Servant
We cannot be here and there too. Cheerly, boys, be brisk a while, and the longer liver take all.

Enter CAPULET, with JULIET and others of his house, meeting the Guests and Maskers

CAPULET
Welcome, gentlemen! ladies that have their toes
Unplagued with corns will have a bout with you.
Ah, my mistresses, which of you all
Will now deny to dance? She that makes dainty,
She I'll swear hath corns. Am I come near ye now?
Welcome, gentlemen! I have seen the day
That I have worn a visor and could tell
A whispering tale in a fair lady's ear,
Such as would please: 'tis gone, 'tis gone, 'tis gone.

ACT I SCENE V. A hall in Capulet's house.

Musicians waiting. Enter Servingmen with napkins

First Servant
Where's Mr Potpan? Why isn't he helping us clear up? He
Should clear the plates. He should wash the plates.

Second Servant
When it's left to just one or two men
to clear up, and they're not that good, it's not a good thing.

First Servant
Take away the stools. Remove the
sideboard. Careful with the plates. Please save
me a piece of marzipan. And, if you would, tell
the guard to let in Susan Grindstone and Nell.
Antony! Potpan!

Second Servant
Yes, sir, we're here.

First Servant
You've been looked for and called for, asked after and
searched for in the great hall.

Second Servant
We can't be in two places at once. Come on, boys, look
lively. Whoever's here the longest gets everything.

Enter CAPULET, with JULIET and others of his house, meeting the Guests and Maskers

CAPULET
Good evening, gentlemen! Ladies that don't
suffer from corns will want to dance with you.
Ah, hello ladies! Which of you
Will refuse to dance? Whoever says she won't
I'll say she has corns. Am I right?
Hello, gentlemen! In the old days,
I'd have worn a mask and would have
Whispered into a lady's ear
To make her smile. Not any more, not any more.

You are welcome, gentlemen. Come, musicians, play.
A hall, a hall, give room! and foot it, girls.

Music plays, and they dance

More light, you knaves, and turn the tables up;
And quench the fire, the room is grown too hot.
Ah, sirrah, this unlooked-for sport comes well.
Nay, sit, nay, sit, good cousin Capulet,
For you and I are past our dancing days.
How long is't now since last yourself and I
Were in a mask?

Second Capulet
Berlady, thirty years.

CAPULET
What, man, 'tis not so much, 'tis not so much:
'Tis since the nuptials of Lucentio,
Come Pentecost as quickly as it will,
Some five and twenty years, and then we masked.

Second Capulet
'Tis more, 'tis more, his son is elder, sir;
His son is thirty.

CAPULET
Will you tell me that?
His son was but a ward two years ago.

ROMEO
[To a Servingman] What lady's that, which doth enrich the hand
Of yonder knight?

Servant
I know not, sir.

Welcome, gentlemen! Come on, musicians, play music.
To the hall, to the hall! Give them room! Off you go, girls.

Music plays, and they dance

Get more light, men. Put the tables away
And put out the fire - the room is getting too hot.
Ah, sir, all this unexpected revelry is going well.
No, please sit down, cousin -
Our dancing days are behind us.
How long is it now since you and I last
Danced at a ball?

Second Capulet
It must be thirty years.

CAPULET
What! Not it can't be, it can't be.
It was at Lucentio's wedding.
The anniversary of which is 50 days after Easter -
That means it's only twenty five years since we danced.

Second Capulet
It's more than that. It's more than that - his son's older, sir.
His son is thirty.

CAPULET
Really?
His son was only a boy two years ago.

ROMEO
[To a Servingman] Who's that lady who is
Holding the hand
Of that knight?

Servant
I don't know, sir.

ROMEO
O she doth teach the torches to burn bright!
It seems she hangs upon the cheek of night
As a rich jewel in an Ethiope's ear -
Beauty too rich for use, for earth too dear:
So shows a snowy dove trooping with crows,
As yonder lady o'er her fellows shows.
The measure done, I'll watch her place of stand,
And touching hers, make blessed my rude hand.
Did my heart love till now? forswear it, sight!
For I ne'er saw true beauty till this night.

TYBALT
This, by his voice, should be a Montague.
Fetch me my rapier, boy. What dares the slave
Come hither, covered with an antic face,
To fleer and scorn at our solemnity?
Now by the stock and honour of my kin,
To strike him dead I hold it not a sin.

CAPULET
Why, how now, kinsman, wherefore storm you so?

TYBALT
Uncle, this is a Montague, our foe:
A villain that is hither come in spite,
To scorn at our solemnity this night.

CAPULET
Young Romeo is it?

TYBALT
'Tis he, that villain Romeo.

CAPULET
Content thee, gentle coz, let him alone,
'A bears him like a portly gentleman;
And to say truth, Verona brags of him
To be a virtuous and well-governed youth.
I would not for the wealth of all the town
Here in my house do him disparagement:
Therefore be patient, take no note of him;
It is my will, the which if thou respect,
Show a fair presence, and put off these frowns,
And ill-beseeming semblance for a feast.

ROMEO
She makes everything seem brighter!
She seems to brighten up the night
Like a jewel hanging from a rich Prince's ear.
Too beautiful to be allowed, too precious to be real!
Like a white dove amongst a gang of crows
Is how she seems when compared with those around her.
The dance is over. I'll watch where she goes
And dare to touch her hand with mine.
Is it possible I was in love before? It cannot be!
Because I never saw anyone as beautiful as her before.

TYBALT
I recognise his voice - he's a Montague.
Get my sword, you. How dare he
Come here, hiding behind a mask,
To sneer and scorn at our party?
To protect the honour and dignity of my family,
I would be justified in killing him.

CAPULET
What's up with you, Tybalt? Why are you so angry?

TYBALT
Uncle, that man is a Montague - our enemy -
Who has come here to spite us
And to sneer at our entertainment tonight.

CAPULET
Is it Romeo?

TYBALT
It is. That good-for-nothing Romeo.

CAPULET
Calm down, Tybalt, and leave him alone.
He behaves like a dignified gentleman
And, if truth be told, people say he is
A very honest and well-behaved young man.
I wouldn't, for anything in the world,
Want to cause him harm in my house.
So calm down and take no notice of him.
Do as I say. If you have any respect for me,
Be civil and stop getting so wound up.
It's not appropriate for a party.

TYBALT
It fits when such a villain is a guest:
I'll not endure him.

CAPULET
He shall be endured.
What, goodman boy, I say he shall, go to!
Am I the master here, or you? go to!
You'll not endure him? God shall mend my soul,
You'll make a mutiny among my guests!
You will set cock-a-hoop! you'll be the man!

TYBALT
Why, uncle, 'tis a shame.

CAPULET
Go to, go to,
You are a saucy boy. Is't so indeed?
This trick may chance to scathe you, I know what.
You must contrary me! Marry, 'tis time -
Well said, my hearts! - You are a princox, go,
Be quiet, or - More light, more light! - For shame,
I'll make you quiet, what! - Cheerly, my hearts!

TYBALT
Patience perforce with wilful choler meeting
Makes my flesh tremble in their different greeting:
I will withdraw, but this intrusion shall,
Now seeming sweet, convert to bitt'rest gall.

Exit

ROMEO
[To JULIET] If I profane with my unworthiest hand
This holy shrine, the gentle fine is this,
My lips, two blushing pilgrims, ready stand
To smooth that rough touch with a tender kiss.

JULIET
Good pilgrim, you do wrong your hand too much,
Which mannerly devotion shows in this,
For saints have hands that pilgrims' hands do touch,
And palm to palm is holy palmers' kiss.

TYBALT
It's appropriate when there's someone like him here.
I won't stand for it.

CAPULET
Yes, you will.
What is it with you? I said, you will. Now, go.
Who's in charge here? Me or you? Go on.
You won't stand for it?! God help me!
You want to cause trouble at my party!
You'll cause uproar! It'll be all down to you!

TYBALT
But, uncle, the shame.

CAPULET
Enough, enough.
You're a bad boy. You think
That he's doing it to annoy you and so
You dare defy me! After all these years -
And it's been many. You are too hot-headed. Go on.
Calm down or - More lights, more lights - Shame on you!
I'll make you behave, I swear. Carry on, everyone!

TYBALT
I am being forced to control my anger.
And, even though it makes me quiver with rage,
I will go. But this insult will -
Though it seems he's got away with it - not be forgotten.

Exit

ROMEO
[To JULIET] I hope you're not offended by my hand
Touching yours. I just want to say this:
My lips, like two young lovers, are willing
To make up for my faux pas with a kiss.

JULIET
Sir, you're being unfair to your hand -
Which you'll realise if you think about it.
Even saints have hands that unworthy people touch.
And hands touching is their equivalent of a kiss.

ROMEO
Have not saints lips, and holy palmers too?

JULIET
Ay, pilgrim, lips that they must use in prayer.

ROMEO
O then, dear saint, let lips do what hands do:
They pray, grant thou, lest faith turn to despair.

JULIET
Saints do not move, though grant for prayers' sake.

ROMEO
Then move not while my prayer's effect I take.
Thus from my lips, by thine, my sin is purged.

JULIET
Then have my lips the sin that they have took.

ROMEO
Sin from thy lips? O trespass sweetly urged!
Give me my sin again.

JULIET
You kiss by th'book.

NURSE
Madam, your mother craves a word with you.

ROMEO
What is her mother?

NURSE
Marry, bachelor,
Her mother is the lady of the house,
And a good lady, and a wise and virtuous.
I nursed her daughter that you talked withal;
I tell you, he that can lay hold of her
Shall have the chinks.

ROMEO
Don't saints have lips? And unworthy people too?

JULIET
Yes - lips which they use to say prayers.

ROMEO
In that case, saint, let our lips do what our hands are doing.
And pray, if you will, that my hope won't turn to despair.

JULIET
But saints won't be moved, unless to grant a prayer.

ROMEO
Then don't move while I answer my prayer.
And my lips, by kissing yours, will be rid of sin.

JULIET
Then my lips have taken that sin.

ROMEO
You've taken sin from thy lips? Oh, what a terrible thing!
Give me my sin back again.

JULIET
You kiss very courteously.

NURSE
Juliet, your mother wants a word with you.

ROMEO
Who is her mother?

NURSE
Young man,
Her mother is the wife of the owner of this house.
She is a good lady, and clever and honest.
I cared for her daughter that you were talking with.
I tell you – the man that manages to win her
Will be very well off.

ROMEO
Is she a Capulet?
O dear account! my life is my foe's debt.

BENVOLIO
Away, be gone, the sport is at the best.

ROMEO
Ay, so I fear, the more is my unrest.

CAPULET
Nay, gentlemen, prepare not to be gone,
We have a trifling foolish banquet towards.
Is it e'en so? Why then I thank you all
I thank you, honest gentlemen, good night.
More torches here, come on! then let's to bed.
Ah, sirrah, by my fay, it waxes late,
I'll to my rest.

Exeunt all but JULIET and Nurse

JULIET
Come hither, Nurse. What is yond gentleman?

NURSE
The son and heir of old Tiberio.

JULIET
What's he that now is going out of door?

NURSE
Marry, that I think be young Petruchio.

JULIET
What's he that follows there, that would not dance?

NURSE
I know not.

JULIET
Go ask his name. - if he be marrièd,
My grave is like to be my wedding bed.

ROMEO
Is she a Capulet?
Oh, dear God! I've given my heart to my enemy.

BENVOLIO
Come on, let's go. We've done all we can here.

ROMEO
Yes, I know. That's what troubles me.

CAPULET
No, gentlemen, don't rush off -
We still have some food left.
Are you sure? In that case, thank you .
Thank you for coming, gentlemen. Good night.
Get more light! Come on! And then let's go to bed.
Ah, sir, I can tell it's getting late.
I'm going to bed.

Exeunt all but JULIET and Nurse

JULIET
Come here, Nurse. Who is that gentleman?

NURSE
Tiberio's son.

JULIET
Who's that just going out of door?

NURSE
I think that's young Petruchio.

JULIET
And who's that following him, who wouldn't dance?

NURSE
I don't know.

JULIET
Go and ask him his name. If he's married
Then I might as well be dead.

NURSE
His name is Romeo, and a Montague,
The only son of your great enemy.

JULIET
My only love sprung from my only hate!
Too early seen unknown, and known too late!
Prodigious birth of love it is to me,
That I must love a loathèd enemy.

NURSE
What's tis? what's tis?

JULIET
A rhyme I learnt even now
Of one I danced withal.

One calls within 'Juliet.'

NURSE
Anon, anon!
Come, let's away; the strangers all are gone.

Exeunt

NURSE
His name is Romeo, and he's a Montague -
The only son of your father's enemy.

JULIET
I've fallen in love with the only person I should hate!
I saw him before I knew, and found out too late!
This new-found love is a terrible thing,
If it means I love an enemy.

NURSE
What's all this?

JULIET
A rhyme I just learned
From someone I danced with.

One calls within 'Juliet.'

NURSE
I'm coming! I'm coming!
Come on, let's go - everyone's leaving.

Exeunt

ACT II

PROLOGUE

Enter Chorus

CHORUS
Now old desire doth in his death-bed lie,
And young affection gapes to be his heir;
That fair for which love groaned for and would die,
With tender Juliet matched is now not fair.
Now Romeo is beloved, and loves again,
Alike bewitchèd by the charm of looks;
But to his foe supposed he must complain,
And she steal love's sweet bait from fearful hooks.
Being held a foe, he may not have access
To breathe such vows as lovers use to swear,
And she as much in love, her means much less
To meet her new-belovèd any where:
But passion lends them power, time means, to meet,
Tempering extremities with extreme sweet.

Exit

ACT II

PROLOGUE

Enter Chorus

CHORUS
Now previous feelings are gone
And new affections spring up in their place.
Although previously his love was unrequited,
With Juliet it's now reciprocated.
She loves Romeo and he loves her -
They're each attracted by the other's looks.
But he must still pretend to hate the Capulets,
And she must love without her family knowing.
As he's the enemy, he can't get near her
To say the things that lovers usually say to each other.
She is just as much in love and it's even harder for her
To meet her darling Romeo anywhere.
But love gives them strength and the opportunity to meet.
So they'll endure the difficulties for their time together.

Exit

ACT II SCENE I. A lane by Capulet's orchard wall.

Enter ROMEO

ROMEO
Can I go forward when my heart is here?
Turn back, dull earth, and find thy centre out.

He climbs the wall, and leaps down within it

Enter BENVOLIO and MERCUTIO

BENVOLIO
Romeo! my cousin Romeo! Romeo!

MERCUTIO
He is wise,
And on my life hath stol'n him home to bed.

BENVOLIO
He ran this way and leapt this orchard wall.
Call, good Mercutio.

MERCUTIO
Nay, I'll conjure too.
Romeo! humours! madman! passion! lover!
Appear thou in the likeness of a sigh,
Speak but one rhyme, and I am satisfied;
Cry but 'Ay me!', pronounce but 'love' and 'dove',
Speak to my gossip Venus one fair word,
One nickname for her purblind son and heir,
Young Abraham Cupid, he that shot so trim
When King Cophetua loved the beggar-maid.
He heareth not, he stirreth not, he moveth not;
The ape is dead, and I must conjure him.
I conjure thee by Rosaline's bright eyes,
By her high forehead and her scarlet lip,
By her fine foot, straight leg, and quivering thigh
And the demesnes that there adjacent lie,
That in thy likeness thou appear to us.

ACT II SCENE I. A lane by Capulet's orchard wall.

Enter ROMEO

ROMEO
How can I leave when my heart wants to stay here?
Turn back, you idiot, and get what you want.

He climbs the wall, and leaps down within it

Enter BENVOLIO and MERCUTIO

BENVOLIO
Romeo! Oh, Romeo!

MERCUTIO
He's a smart man.
I'll bet he's gone home to bed.

BENVOLIO
He came this way and leapt over the orchard wall.
Call to him, Mercutio.

MERCUTIO
No, I'll magic him.
Romeo! You witty, crazy, passionate lover!
Make yourself known by sighing.
Say just one word and we'll be happy.
Say only 'Oh dear!' Say the words 'love' and 'dove'
Ask the goddess Venus for help,
Call out the name of her son who is believed to be blind -
Young Cupid - who supposedly could make,
A king love a beggar-maid!
He can't hear. He hasn't responded. He isn't moving.
He must be playing dead. I will make him appear.
I'll use Rosaline's beautiful eyes,
Her high forehead and her scarlet lips,
Her pretty feet, long legs and attractive thigh,
And everything else that's close to it.
That will make you appear!

BENVOLIO
And if he hear thee, thou wilt anger him.

MERCUTIO
This cannot anger him: 'twould anger him
To raise a spirit in his mistress' circle,
Of some strange nature, letting it there stand
Till she had laid it and conjured it down:
That were some spite. My invocation
Is fair and honest: in his mistress' name
I conjure only but to raise up him.

BENVOLIO
Come, he hath hid himself among these trees
To be consorted with the humorous night:
Blind is his love, and best befits the dark.

MERCUTIO
If love be blind, love cannot hit the mark.
Now will he sit under a medlar tree,
And wish his mistress were that kind of fruit
As maids call medlars, when they laugh alone.
O Romeo, that she were, O that she were
An open-arse, thou a pop'rin pear!
Romeo, good night, I'll to my truckle-bed,
This field-bed is too cold for me to sleep.
Come, shall we go?

BENVOLIO
Go, then, for 'tis in vain
To seek him here that means not to be found.

Exeunt

BENVOLIO
If he can hear you, he'll be very angry.

MERCUTIO
This won't make him angry. It would make him angry
If someone else got to sleep with Rosaline
Somehow. And she let them
And laid down and let them finish.
That would upset him. My 'spell'
Is simple but honest. By using Rosaline's name
I'm only trying to coax him out.

BENVOLIO
He's hidden himself amongst the trees
To be concealed in the shadows.
Love is blind, which is best suited to darkness.

MERCUTIO
If love is blind, it cannot truly strike.
Now he'll sit in a tree,
And wish that Rosaline was the type of fruit
Woman call medlars when they talk among themselves.
Romeo will wish she was - oh, if only she was -
A ripe fruit that he might pluck!
Good night, Romeo. I'm going to bed.
It's too cold to sleep in this field.
Come on, let's go.

BENVOLIO
Alright. There's no point
In looking for him if he doesn't want to be found.

Exeunt

ACT II SCENE II. Capulet's orchard.

Enter ROMEO

ROMEO
He jests at scars that never felt a wound.

JULIET appears above at a window

But, soft, what light through yonder window breaks?
It is the east, and Juliet is the sun.
Arise, fair sun, and kill the envious moon,
Who is already sick and pale with grief
That thou, her maid, art far more fair than she.
Be not her maid, since she is envious;
Her vestal livery is but sick and green,
And none but fools do wear it; cast it off.
It is my lady, O, it is my love:
O that she knew she were!
She speaks, yet she says nothing; what of that?
Her eye discourses, I will answer it.
I am too bold, 'tis not to me she speaks:
Two of the fairest stars in all the heaven,
Having some business, do entreat her eyes
To twinkle in their spheres till they return.
What if her eyes were there, they in her head?
The brightness of her cheek would shame those stars,
As daylight doth a lamp; her eyes in heaven
Would through the airy region stream so bright
That birds would sing and think it were not night.
See how she leans her cheek upon her hand!
O that I were a glove upon that hand,
That I might touch that cheek!

JULIET
Ay me!

ROMEO
She speaks.
O speak again, bright angel, for thou art
As glorious to this night, being o'er my head,
As is a winged messenger of heaven
Unto the white-upturned wond'ring eyes
Of mortals that fall back to gaze on him,

ACT II SCENE II. Capulet's orchard.

Enter ROMEO

ROMEO
What do they know about love?

JULIET appears above at a window

Wait! What's that light coming through that window?
It's Juliet - who shines like the sun.
Come out here, dear Juliet, and outshine the moon,
Which pales into insignificance
As you - a human - are far more beautiful than it.
Don't let it bother you - the moon is just jealous.
You can tell from looking at it.
No-one wants to be like that - ignore it.
It's her! It's the woman I love!
Oh, if only she knew she was!
She seems about to speak but yet doesn't. I wonder why.
Her eyes speak to me - I want to answer their call.
But that's foolish. It's not me they're looking at.
Two of the brightest stars in the sky,
For some reason, have captured her attention -
Their reflections twinkle in her eyes.
Even if her eyes were stars and she had stars in her head
The beauty of her face would still outshine them
Like sunlight outshines a light bulb. If her eyes were stars
They'd make the sky seem so bright
That birds would sing because they'd think it was daytime.
Look how she's leaning her cheek on her hand.
Oh, I wish I was a glove on that hand,
So I could touch her cheek.

JULIET
Oh, dear!

ROMEO
She spoke!
Oh, please speak again, beautiful angel! Because you are
As wondrous a sight to behold
As when an angel of heaven
Appears to people on earth
Who gaze up at them

When he bestrides the lazy puffing clouds,
And sails upon the bosom of the air.

JULIET
O Romeo, Romeo, wherefore art thou Romeo?
Deny thy father and refuse thy name;
Or, if thou wilt not, be but sworn my love,
And I'll no longer be a Capulet.

ROMEO
[Aside] Shall I hear more, or shall I speak at this?

JULIET
'Tis but thy name that is my enemy;
Thou art thyself, though not a Montague.
What's Montague? It is nor hand, nor foot,
Nor arm nor face, nor any other part
Belonging to a man. O be some other name!
What's in a name? That which we call a rose
By any other word would smell as sweet;
So Romeo would, were he not Romeo called,
Retain that dear perfection which he owes
Without that title. Romeo, doff thy name,
And for thy name, which is no part of thee,
Take all myself.

ROMEO
I take thee at thy word:
Call me but love, and I'll be new baptized;
Henceforth I never will be Romeo.

JULIET
What man art thou that thus bescreened in night
So stumblest on my counsel?

ROMEO
By a name
I know not how to tell thee who I am.
My name, dear saint, is hateful to myself,
Because it is an enemy to thee;
Had I it written, I would tear the word.

As they sit upon clouds
And drift through the air.

JULIET
Oh, Romeo, Romeo! Why did you have to be Romeo?
Renounce your family and change your name.
Or, if you won't, just promise you love me
And I won't be a Capulet any more.

ROMEO
[Aside] Should I wait to hear more or should I speak now?

JULIET
It's only your surname that's a problem.
But you are you and not your name.
What's Montague? It's not the hand, or foot,
Or arm, or face, or any other part
Of a man's body. Oh, if only you had a different surname!
Why should a name matter? If we called a rose
Something else it would still smell the same.
So Romeo would, even if he wasn't called Romeo,
Still be as wonderful as he is now
Even without that name. Romeo, get rid of your name.
And, in return for getting rid of a name which isn't you,
You can have me.

ROMEO
I agree to do what you say.
Tell me you love me and I'll be a new man.
From now on I'll never be called Romeo again.

JULIET
Who is that who hidden in the shadows
Is eavesdropping on my thoughts?

ROMEO
My name
I don't know how to tell you.
My name, my darling, is something I hate
Because it causes you problems.
If I had it written down, I would tear it into pieces.

JULIET
My ears have not yet drunk a hundred words
Of thy tongue's uttering, yet I know the sound:
Art thou not Romeo, and a Montague?

ROMEO
Neither, fair maid, if either thee dislike.

JULIET
How cam'st thou hither, tell me, and wherefore?
The orchard walls are high and hard to climb,
And the place death, considering who thou art,
If any of my kinsmen find thee here.

ROMEO
With love's light wings did I o'er-perch these walls,
For stony limits cannot hold love out,
And what love can do, that dares love attempt:
Therefore thy kinsmen are no stop to me.

JULIET
If they do see thee, they will murder thee.

ROMEO
Alack, there lies more peril in thine eye
Than twenty of their swords. Look thou but sweet,
And I am proof against their enmity.

JULIET
I would not for the world they saw thee here.

ROMEO
I have night's cloak to hide me from their eyes,
And but thou love me, let them find me here;
My life were better ended by their hate,
Than death prorogued, wanting of thy love.

JULIET
By whose direction found'st thou out this place?

JULIET
Even though less than a hundred words
Have been spoken, I recognise your voice.
Aren't you Romeo - a Montague?

ROMEO
No, darling - not if you don't want me to be.

JULIET
How did you get here? Tell me. And why have you come?
The orchard walls are high and hard to climb.
And this place is dangerous considering who you are.
Especially if any of my family find you here.

ROMEO
The power of love helped me over the walls
Because even they cannot keep love out,
Or stop what love can do and what lovers dare to do.
So your family don't scare me.

JULIET
If they see you, they will kill you.

ROMEO
But your beauty gives me more strength
Than twenty of them. If you just look at me kindly,
I will have enough strength to fight them all.

JULIET
I really hope they don't find you here.

ROMEO
The darkness will keep me hidden from them.
But, if you don't love me, then let them find me here.
I'd rather let them kill me
Than be tormented longing for your love.

JULIET
How did you know how to get here?

ROMEO
By Love, who first did prompt me to enquire;
He lent me counsel, and I lent him eyes.
I am no pilot, yet wert thou as far
As that vast shore washed with the farthest sea,
I would adventure for such merchandise.

JULIET
Thou knowest the mask of night is on my face,
Else would a maiden blush bepaint my cheek
For that which thou hast heard me speak tonight
Fain would I dwell on form, fain, fain deny
What I have spoke, but farewell compliment!
Dost thou love me? I know thou wilt say 'Ay';
And I will take thy word; yet if thou swear'st,
Thou mayst prove false: at lovers' perjuries
They say Jove laughs. O gentle Romeo,
If thou dost love, pronounce it faithfully;
Or if thou think'st I am too quickly won,
I'll frown and be perverse and say thee nay,
So thou wilt woo, but else not for the world.
In truth, fair Montague, I am too fond,
And therefore thou mayst think my behaviour light:
But trust me, gentleman, I'll prove more true
Than those that have more coying to be strange.
I should have been more strange, I must confess,
But that thou overheard'st, ere I was ware,
My true love's passion; therefore pardon me,
And not impute this yielding to light love,
Which the dark night hath so discovered.

ROMEO
Lady, by yonder blessèd moon I vow,
That tips with silver all these fruit-tree tops –

JULIET
O swear not by the moon, th'inconstant moon,
That monthly changes in her circled orb,
Lest that thy love prove likewise variable.

ROMEO
What shall I swear by?

ROMEO
Love, which first motivated me to find you,
Guided me and I let it.
I'm not a traveller but, even if you were as far away
As the furthest land across the furthest sea,
I would still travel to see you.

JULIET
It's good the darkness of the night is obscuring my face
Otherwise you'd see me blushing.
To think you heard what I said tonight.
I wish I could retain my composure, wish I could deny
What I said. But it's too late for that.
Do you love me? I know you will say 'Yes'
And I will believe you. But if you swear it
You may still turn out to be lying. Lovers' lies
Are all too common. Oh, please, Romeo,
If you do love me, say so honestly.
Or, if you think I'm being too easy,
I'll withdraw and be awkward and say I don't
So you will have to woo me - which I don't want to do.
To be honest, Romeo, I like you too much.
Therefore you might think my feelings are unsubstantial
But believe me, Romeo, I'll prove they're more sincere
Than those that are more able to seem coy.
I should have been more coy, I admit.
But as you overheard, before I knew you were here,
What I truly feel, I hope you'll forgive me
And not put down to insubstantial feelings my willingness,
Which you discovered whilst hidden by the darkness.

ROMEO
Juliet, I swear by the moon -
Whose light touches the treetops…

JULIET
Don't swear by the moon - it's not steadfast
It changes every month as it rotates.
Unless that means your love is equally changeable.

ROMEO
What should I swear by?

JULIET
Do not swear at all;
Or if thou wilt, swear by thy gracious self,
Which is the god of my idolatry,
And I'll believe thee.

ROMEO
If my heart's dear love -

JULIET
Well, do not swear. Although I joy in thee,
I have no joy of this contract tonight:
It is too rash, too unadvised, too sudden,
Too like the lightning, which doth cease to be
Ere one can say 'It lightens'. Sweet, good night:
This bud of love, by summer's ripening breath,
May prove a beauteous flower when next we meet.
Good night, good night! as sweet repose and rest
Come to thy heart as that within my breast.

ROMEO
O wilt thou leave me so unsatisfied?

JULIET
What satisfaction canst thou have tonight?

ROMEO
Th'exchange of thy love's faithful vow for mine.

JULIET
I gave thee mine before thou didst request it;
And yet I would it were to give again.

ROMEO
Wouldst thou withdraw it? for what purpose, love?

JULIET
But to be frank, and give it thee again.
And yet I wish but for the thing I have:
My bounty is as boundless as the sea,
My love as deep; the more I give to thee
The more I have, for both are infinite.

Nurse calls within

JULIET
Don't swear at all.
Or, if you want to, swear on your life,
Which is the focus of my love,
And I'll believe you.

ROMEO
With all my heart…

JULIET
Yes, that'll do. Although I enjoy seeing you,
I don't enjoy you being here tonight.
It is too hasty, too risky, too sudden,
Too much like lightning, which is gone
Before you can say 'It's lightning.' Good night, darling!
Our blossoming love, which is blooming in the summer,
Might become something beautiful when we next meet.
Good night, good night! I wish the same feeling of peace
To you as that which you instil in me.

ROMEO
You'd leave me without reassurance of your feelings?

JULIET
What more reassurance could you have?

ROMEO
For us to both swear we love each other.

JULIET
I already did before you asked me to.
Although I wish I could take it back.

ROMEO
You want to take it back? But why, darling?

JULIET
So I could, in all honesty, say it again.
And thus I wish for something I already have.
I am as willing to say it as the sea is wide,
My love is just as deep. The more I give to you,
The more I have because we both feel the same.

Nurse calls within

I hear some noise within; dear love, adieu!
Anon, good Nurse! - Sweet Montague, be true.
Stay but a little, I will come again.

Exit, above

ROMEO
O blessèd, blessèd night! I am afeard,
Being in night, all this is but a dream,
Too flattering-sweet to be substantial.

Re-enter JULIET, above

JULIET
Three words, dear Romeo, and good night indeed.
If that thy bent of love be honourable,
Thy purpose marriage, send me word tomorrow,
By one that I'll procure to come to thee,
Where and what time thou wilt perform the rite,
And all my fortunes at thy foot I'll lay,
And follow thee my lord throughout the world.

NURSE
[Within] Madam!

JULIET
I come, anon. - But if thou meanest not well,
I do beseech thee -

NURSE
[Within] Madam!

JULIET
By and by I come -
To cease thy strife, and leave me to my grief.
Tomorrow will I send.

ROMEO
So thrive my soul -

JULIET
A thousand times good night!

Exit, above

I can hear someone calling. Goodnight, my darling!
I'm coming, Nurse! My darling Romeo, be patient.
Wait a bit longer, I will come back.

Exit, above

ROMEO
Oh, what a wonderful night! I am worried
That, as this is night, it might all be a dream.
It's too wonderful to be true.

Re-enter JULIET, above

JULIET
Three last words, dear Romeo, and then I've got to go.
If your feelings are honourable
And you intend marriage, send me a message tomorrow -
By someone who I'll arrange to come find you -
Where and what time the ceremony is to take place
And I'll give you all that I have
And follow you throughout my whole life.

NURSE
[Within] Juliet!

JULIET
I'm coming, wait. – But, if you don't mean to marry me,
Then I beg you -

NURSE
[Within] Juliet!

JULIET
All right, all right, I'm coming -
To stop pursuing me, and leave me in peace.
Tomorrow I will send someone to find you.

ROMEO
I can't wait.

JULIET
I wish you good night a thousand times!

Exit, above

ROMEO
A thousand times the worse, to want thy light.
Love goes toward love as schoolboys from their books,
But love from love, toward school with heavy looks.

Retiring

Re-enter JULIET, above

JULIET
Hist, Romeo, hist! O for a falconer's voice,
To lure this tassel-gentle back again:
Bondage is hoarse, and may not speak aloud,
Else would I tear the cave where Echo lies,
And make her airy tongue more hoarse than mine
With repetition of my Romeo's name.

ROMEO
It is my soul that calls upon my name.
How silver-sweet sound lovers' tongues by night,
Like softest music to attending ears!

JULIET
Romeo!

ROMEO
My niesse?

JULIET
At what a'clock tomorrow
Shall I send to thee?

ROMEO
By the hour of nine.

JULIET
I will not fail, 'tis twenty year till then.
I have forgot why I did call thee back.

ROMEO
Let me stand here till thou remember it.

ROMEO
And I'm a thousand times worse off without you.
I'd go towards you happily like a schoolboy leaving school,
But leave you as reluctantly as a schoolboy goes to school.

Retiring

Re-enter JULIET, above

JULIET
Hey! Romeo! Hey! Oh, I wish I knew how
To call him back again!
I'm constrained by our situation and can't call out loud.
Otherwise I'd yell as loud as I can
And make my echo sound hoarse from all my yelling
Romeo's name.

ROMEO
And yet I felt you calling me.
How beautiful your voice sounds -
Like music to my ears!

JULIET
Romeo,

ROMEO
My dear?

JULIET
What time tomorrow
Should I send someone to find you?

ROMEO
At nine o'clock.

JULIET
I won't forget. It'll seem like twenty years until then.
I've forgotten why I called you back.

ROMEO
Let me wait here while you remember it.

JULIET
I shall forget, to have thee still stand there,
Remembering how I love thy company.

ROMEO
And I'll still stay, to have thee still forget,
Forgetting any other home but this.

JULIET
'Tis almost morning, I would have thee gone:
And yet no farther than a wanton's bird,
That lets it hop a little from her hand,
Like a poor prisoner in his twisted gyves,
And with a silken thread plucks it back again,
So loving-jealous of his liberty.

ROMEO
I would I were thy bird.

JULIET
Sweet, so would I,
Yet I should kill thee with much cherishing.
Good night, good night! Parting is such
sweet sorrow,
That I shall say good night till it be morrow.

Exit above

ROMEO
Sleep dwell upon thine eyes, peace in thy breast!
Would I were sleep and peace, so sweet to rest!
Hence will I to my ghostly sire's close cell,
His help to crave, and my dear hap to tell.

Exit

JULIET
I'll keep forgetting if you're standing there
Because I'll think about how much I love being with you.

ROMEO
And I'll keep waiting so you can keep forgetting.
And we can stay here forever.

JULIET
It's almost morning. You'd better go.
But no further than a faithful pet bird
When it is allowed to stray from its owner's hand
But is restrained by its shackles,
Which easily draw it back again
Because the owner misses it so much.

ROMEO
I wish I could be your pet.

JULIET
I wish you could be too.
But I would kill you with kindness.
Good night, good night! Saying goodbye is
Wonderful and yet horrible,
But I must say good night for now.

Exit above

ROMEO
I hope you sleep well and peacefully.
And I wish I could sleep so easily.
Now I'll go to Friar Lawrence,
To ask for his help and tell him what has happened.

Exit

ACT II SCENE III. Friar Lawrence's cell.

Enter FRIAR LAWRENCE, with a basket

FRIAR LAWRENCE
The grey-eyed morn smiles on the frowning night,
Check'ring the eastern clouds with streaks of light;
And flecked darkness like a drunkard reels
From forth day's path and Titan's fiery wheels:
Now ere the sun advance his burning eye,
The day to cheer, and night's dank dew to dry,
I must upfill this osier cage of ours
With baleful weeds and precious-juicèd flowers.
The earth that's nature's mother is her tomb;
What is her burying grave, that is her womb;
And from her womb children of divers kind
We sucking on her natural bosom find:
Many for many virtues excellent,
None but for some, and yet all different.
O mickle is the powerful grace that lies
In plants, herbs, stones, and their true qualities:
For nought so vile that on the earth doth live,
But to the earth some special good doth give,
Nor ought so good but, strained from that fair use,
Revolts from true birth, stumbling on abuse.
Virtue itself turns vice, being misapplied,
And vice sometimes by action dignified.
Within the infant rind of this small flower
Poison hath residence, and medicine power:
For this, being smelt, with that part cheers each part,
Being tasted, slays all senses with the heart.
Two such opposèd kings encamp them still
In man as well as herbs, grace and rude will;
And where the worser is predominant,
Full soon the canker death eats up that plant.

Enter ROMEO

ROMEO
Good morrow, father.

ACT II SCENE III. Friar Lawrence's cell.

Enter FRIAR LAWRENCE, with a basket

FRIAR LAWRENCE
The morning is slowly replacing the night -
Shining on the clouds with streaks of light.
And getting rid of darkness which seems to run unsteadily
Away from the day and its light,
Which is beginning to shine in the sky
To cheer everyone up and dry the dew.
I must fill this wicker basket of mine
With poisonous but useful plants.
The earth in which nature is buried
Might be thought of as its grave but it also gives life
As, from the earth, various things grow
Which we find are nurtured by the earth -
Many of which have many good qualities,
Only some have none and they're all different.
There is a great amount of power to be found
In herbs, plants, stones, and everything they can do
And there's nothing on the earth that's so vile
That it can't be used to help the earth.
Nor anything so beneficial that if pushed to extremes
Would reject its goodness – having been corrupted by evil.
Goodness can become evil if it is misused.
And what is thought evil might sometimes be necessary.
Within the skin of this small flower
Can be found both poison and pleasantness
Because, if you were to smell it, you'd like it,
But if you ate it, it would kill you.
Two such opposite natures can be found
In men as well as plants – goodness and wickedness -
And, when the worse one is stronger,
It soon takes over its entire being.

Enter ROMEO

ROMEO
Hello Friar Lawrence.

FRIAR LAWRENCE
Benedicite!
What early tongue so sweet saluteth me?
Young son, it argues a distempered head
So soon to bid good morrow to thy bed:
Care keeps his watch in every old man's eye,
And where care lodges, sleep will never lie;
But where unbruisèd youth with unstuffed brain
Doth couch his limbs, there golden sleep doth reign.
Therefore thy earliness doth me assure
Thou art up-roused by some distemp'rature;
Or if not so, then here I hit it right,
Our Romeo hath not been in bed tonight.

ROMEO
That last is true, the sweeter rest was mine.

FRIAR LAWRENCE
God pardon sin! wast thou with Rosaline?

ROMEO
With Rosaline, my ghostly father? no;
I have forgot that name, and that name's woe.

FRIAR LAWRENCE
That's my good son, but where hast thou been then?

ROMEO
I'll tell thee ere thou ask it me again:
I have been feasting with mine enemy,
Where on a sudden one hath wounded me,
That's by me wounded; both our remedies
Within thy help and holy physic lies.
I bear no hatred, blessed man; for lo,
My intercession likewise steads my foe.

FRIAR LAWRENCE
Be plain, good son, and homely in thy drift,
Riddling confession finds but riddling shrift.

FRIAR LAWRENCE
Goodness me!
Who is that who's greeting me so early?
My son, it suggests that you are troubled
When you are up so early.
Worries often trouble the old
And those who are troubled find it hard to sleep.
But where unconcerned young men with untroubled minds
Chose to lie down they find it easy to sleep.
Therefore you being up so early makes me think
You've been woken up by something that troubles you
Or, if that's not the case, I think I'm right in saying
You haven't been to bed at all last night.

ROMEO
That last bit's true - I wouldn't have trouble sleeping.

FRIAR LAWRENCE
Good lord! Were you with Rosaline?

ROMEO
With Rosaline, Friar Lawrence? No.
I have forgotten about her - she means nothing to me.

FRIAR LAWRENCE
That's good, my son. But then where have you been?

ROMEO
I'll tell you, before you ask me again -
I've been over at my enemy's house
Where I was suddenly so enamoured by someone
Who was also enamoured by me and the ability to help us
Is within your power and remit.
I don't feel any hatred now, Father, because
What has happened means I no longer have an enemy.

FRIAR LAWRENCE
Speak plainly, my son, and be clear in what you say -
A confusing confession won't get a satisfactory absolution.

ROMEO
Then plainly know my heart's dear love is set
On the fair daughter of rich Capulet;
As mine on hers, so hers is set on mine,
And all combined, save what thou must combine
By holy marriage. When and where and how
We met, we wooed and made exchange of vow,
I'll tell thee as we pass, but this I pray,
That thou consent to marry us today.

FRIAR LAWRENCE
Holy Saint Francis, what a change is here!
Is Rosaline, whom thou didst love so dear,
So soon forsaken? Young men's love then lies
Not truly in their hearts, but in their eyes.
Jesu Maria, what a deal of brine
Hath washed thy sallow cheeks for Rosaline!
How much salt water thrown away in waste,
To season love, that of it doth not taste!
The sun not yet thy sighs from heaven clears,
Thy old groans ring yet in my ancient ears;
Lo here upon thy cheek the stain doth sit
Of an old tear that is not washed off yet:
If e'er thou wast thyself, and these woes thine,
Thou and these woes were all for Rosaline.
And art thou changed? Pronounce this sentence then:
Women may fall, when there's no strength in men.

ROMEO
Thou chid'st me oft for loving Rosaline.

FRIAR LAWRENCE
For doting, not for loving, pupil mine.

ROMEO
And bad'st me bury love.

FRIAR LAWRENCE
Not in a grave,
To lay one in, another out to have.

ROMEO
Then I will tell you that I have fallen in love
With Capulet's daughter.
And, as much I love her, she loves me.
Our hearts are joined and you must join the rest of us
In holy matrimony. When and where and how
We met, fell in love and swore our love,
I'll tell you in due course. But I hope
That you will agree to marry us today.

FRIAR LAWRENCE
Good lord, this is a very sudden!
Is Rosaline, that you seemed to love so much,
Forgotten so quickly? Then, surely, young men's love
Isn't based on what they feel but what they see.
Good grief. There were a lot of tears
Shed by you because of Rosaline.
It seems it was all pointless
And for a love that you never even knew!
It's not yet been a day since you were pining for her
And your moans are still ringing in my ears.
On your cheek there is still a mark
Of a tear that hasn't been washed off yet.
If that really was you and it was you who shed those tears,
Then you were completely set on Rosaline.
And yet you've changed your mind? Then it must be said
That women need to watch out if men are so fickle.

ROMEO
You told me off for being in love with Rosaline.

FRIAR LAWRENCE
For pining for her, not for loving her, Romeo.

ROMEO
And you told me to forget about her.

FRIAR LAWRENCE
Not completely.
Only to put her to one side to find someone else.

ROMEO
I pray thee chide me not; Her I love now
Doth grace for grace and love for love allow;
The other did not so.

FRIAR LAWRENCE
O she knew well
Thy love did read by rote, that could not spell.
But come, young waverer, come go with me,
In one respect I'll thy assistant be:
For this alliance may so happy prove
To turn your households' rancour to pure love.

ROMEO
O let us hence, I stand on sudden haste.

FRIAR LAWRENCE
Wisely and slow, they stumble that run fast.

Exeunt

ROMEO
So please don't scold me. The woman I love now
Reciprocates my feelings and affections.
Rosaline didn't.

FRIAR LAWRENCE
That's because she knew
Your love wasn't real and had no substance.
But come on, young fickle one, come with me.
In one way I'll help you
Because your marriage might help
To stop your families fighting each other.

ROMEO
Yes, let's go. I can't wait any longer.

FRIAR LAWRENCE
Slowly and steadily. People who rush make mistakes.

Exeunt

ACT II SCENE IV. A street.

Enter BENVOLIO and MERCUTIO

MERCUTIO
Where the dev'l should this Romeo be?
Came he not home tonight?

BENVOLIO
Not to his father's, I spoke with his man.

MERCUTIO
Why, that same pale hard-hearted wench, that Rosaline,
Torments him so, that he will sure run mad.

BENVOLIO
Tybalt, the kinsman of old Capulet,
Hath sent a letter to his father's house.

MERCUTIO
A challenge, on my life.

BENVOLIO
Romeo will answer it.

MERCUTIO
Any man that can write may answer a letter.

BENVOLIO
Nay, he will answer the letter's master, how he
dares, being dared.

MERCUTIO
Alas, poor Romeo, he is already dead, stabbed with a
white wench's black eye;,shot through the ear with a
love-song, the very pin of his heart cleft with the
blind bow-boy's butt-shaft; and is he a man to
encounter Tybalt?

BENVOLIO
Why, what is Tybalt?

ACT II SCENE IV. A street.

Enter BENVOLIO and MERCUTIO

MERCUTIO
Where on earth is Romeo?
Did he come home last night?

BENVOLIO
Not to his father's. I spoke to his servant.

MERCUTIO
Ah, that pretty, hard-hearted woman, Rosaline,
Torments him so much that he'll surely go mad.

BENVOLIO
Tybalt, a relative of Capulet's,
Has sent a letter to his father's house.

MERCUTIO
I'll bet it's a challenge.

BENVOLIO
Romeo will respond.

MERCUTIO
Anyone who can write can respond to a letter.

BENVOLIO
No, I mean he'll respond to the letter's writer, however he wants, if he's challenged him.

MERCUTIO
Ah, poor Romeo! He's already dead - killed by a
woman's unkindness, poisoned by
love and shot through the heart by
Cupid's arrow. And you reckon he's fit to
take on Tybalt?

BENVOLIO
Why? What kind of man is Tybalt?

MERCUTIO
More than Prince of Cats. O, he's
the courageous captain of compliments: he fights as
you sing prick-song, keeps time, distance, and
proportion; he rests his minim rests, one, two, and
the third in your bosom; the very butcher of a silk
button, a duellist, a duellist; a gentleman of the
very first house, of the first and second cause.
Ah, the immortal 'passado', the 'punto reverso', the
'hay'!

BENVOLIO
The what?

MERCUTIO
The pox of such antic, lisping, affecting
phantasimes, these new tuners of accent! 'By Jesu,
a very good blade! a very tall man! a very good
whore!' Why, is not this a lamentable thing,
grandsire, that we should be thus afflicted with
these strange flies, these fashion-mongers, these
pardon-me's, who stand so much on the new form,
that they cannot at ease on the old bench? O their
bones, their bones!

Enter ROMEO

BENVOLIO
Here comes Romeo, here comes Romeo.

MERCUTIO
Without his roe, like a dried herring: O flesh, flesh,
how art thou fishified! Now is he for the numbers
that Petrarch flowed in. Laura to his lady was but a
kitchen wench; marry, she had a better love to
be-rhyme her; Dido a dowdy; Cleopatra a gipsy;
Helen and Hero hildings and harlots; Thisbe a grey
eye or so, but not to the purpose. Signior
Romeo, 'bon jour'! there's a French salutation
to your French slop. You gave us the counterfeit
fairly last night.

MERCUTIO
More than a good name for a cat. He is
a very experienced fighter. He fights as
well as you can sing, keeping time, distance, and
correct stance. He'll rest for a moment, one, two, and on
the third strike you in your chest. He's sliced off many
silk buttons. He's a good duellist. A gentleman of the
highest reputation, of the first and second highest skill.
Ah, the famous lunge! The backhanded thrust! The
hit!

BENVOLIO
The what?

MERCUTIO
Who cares about these timid, inarticulate, posturing
young men - these new trendsetters! Yes,
he's a good fighter! A very fine man! Very
worldly! Isn't it a shame,
Benvolio, that we have to put up with
such strange people - the fashion obsessed, the
overly courteous - who are so focused on the new,
that they can't abide the old? To hell
with them all!

Enter ROMEO

BENVOLIO
Here comes Romeo. Look - here comes Romeo.

MERCUTIO
Without his love, he's like a dried up has-been. Poor thing.
To be so ridiculed! To be counted among the
unsuccessful lovers. But then Petarch's Laura was just a
kitchen maid – although he did better at
flattering her. Dido was a nothing. Cleopatra a tramp.
Helen and Hero whores and prostitutes. Thisbe just an
eye in a wall. And not even focused on the right thing.
Bonjour Romeo! I'm greeting you in French
to match your French fashion. You gave us the slip
last night.

ROMEO
Good morrow to you both. What counterfeit did I give you?

MERCUTIO
The ship, sir, the slip, can you not conceive?

ROMEO
Pardon, good Mercutio, my business was great, and in such a case as mine a man may strain courtesy.

MERCUTIO
That's as much as to say, such a case as yours constrains a man to bow in the hams.

ROMEO
Meaning to cur'sey.

MERCUTIO
Thou hast most kindly hit it.

ROMEO
A most courteous exposition.

MERCUTIO
Nay, I am the very pink of courtesy.

ROMEO
Pink for flower.

MERCUTIO
Right.

ROMEO
Why, then is my pump well flowered.

MERCUTIO
Sure wit! Follow me this jest now, till thou hast worn out thy pump, that when the single sole of it is worn, the jest may remain, after the wearing, solely singular.

ROMEO
O single-soled jest, solely singular for the singleness!

ROMEO
Hello, you two. When did I give you the slip?

MERCUTIO
When? When? Can't you remember?

ROMEO
Forgive me, Mercutio, I had important business. And in such cases men are allowed to overlook courtesy.

MERCUTIO
That's the same as saying a case such as yours
means you must bow to pressure.

ROMEO
You mean curtsey.

MERCUTIO
Exactly.

ROMEO
Very pleasantly put.

MERCUTIO
Yes, I am very pleasant

ROMEO
Like a flower.

MERCUTIO
Yes.

ROMEO
In that case my shoe is very pleasant.

MERCUTIO
Very witty. See if you can follow this - until you
get worn out from trying - that even when your shoe
is worn out, the joke will remain - a singular achievement.

ROMEO
A singular joke. Completely alone in its
uniqueness.

MERCUTIO
Come between us, good Benvolio, my wits faint.

ROMEO
Swits and spurs, swits and spurs, or I'll cry a match.

MERCUTIO
Nay, if thy wits run the wild-goose chase, I have
done, for thou hast more of the wild-goose in one of
thy wits than, I am sure, I have in my whole five.
Was I with you there for the goose?

ROMEO
Thou wast never with me for any thing when thou wast
not there for the goose.

MERCUTIO
I will bite thee by the ear for that jest.

ROMEO
Nay, good goose, bite not.

MERCUTIO
Thy wit is a very bitter sweeting, it is a most
sharp sauce.

ROMEO
And is it not well served in to a sweet goose?

MERCUTIO
O here's a wit of cheverel, that stretches from an
inch narrow to an ell broad!

ROMEO
I stretch it out for that word 'broad', which added
to the goose, proves thee far and wide a broad goose.

MERCUTIO
Why, is not this better now than groaning for love?
Now art thou sociable, now art thou Romeo; now art
thou what thou art, by art as well as by nature,
for this drivelling love is like a great natural
that runs lolling up and down to hide his bauble in a hole.

MERCUTIO
Come help me, Benvolio - I'm running out of retorts.

ROMEO
Come on, keep going or I'll say I've won.

MERCUTIO
No, there's no point in it, I'm
finished. For you have more pointlessness in your one
wit than, I know, I have in any of mine.
Did I beat you with that one?

ROMEO
You can't ever beat me if you're not trying
To get points.

MERCUTIO
I will get you back for that.

ROMEO
No, Mr Pointless, please don't.

MERCUTIO
Your wit is bittersweet - it has a
sharpness to it.

ROMEO
In that case it's well used to win points.

MERCUTIO
Oh, what a broad wit – I bet you could keep it
going for hours!

ROMEO
I'll use your comment about 'hours' which, added
to 'pointless', means you've been pointless for hours.

MERCUTIO
Isn't this better than pining after your love?
Now you're being sociable, you're being Romeo, you're
being yourself by showing you natural wit
rather than drivelling about love like an idiot,
stumbling about after a pretty thing you can't have.

BENVOLIO
Stop there, stop there.

MERCUTIO
Thou desirest me to stop in my tale against the hair.

BENVOLIO
Thou wouldst else have made thy tale large.

MERCUTIO
O thou art deceived; I would have made it short, for I was come to the whole depth of my tale, and meant indeed to occupy the argument no longer.

ROMEO
Here's goodly gear!

Enter Nurse and PETER

MERCUTIO
A sail, a sail!

BENVOLIO
Two, two; a shirt and a smock.

NURSE
Peter!

PETER
Anon!

NURSE
My fan, Peter.

MERCUTIO
Good Peter, to hide her face, for her fan's the fairer face.

NURSE
God ye good morrow, gentlemen.

MERCUTIO
God ye good den, fair gentlewoman.

BENVOLIO
Enough, enough.

MERCUTIO
You want me to stop when I'm winning.

BENVOLIO
Otherwise you'd have gone too far.

MERCUTIO
You're wrong. I would have kept it short
Because I'd almost finished – I
didn't intend to go on any longer.

ROMEO
That's good to hear!

Enter Nurse and PETER

MERCUTIO
Look! Who's this?

BENVOLIO
Two. Two of them - a man and a woman.

NURSE
Peter!

PETER
Yes?

NURSE
Get my fan, Peter.

MERCUTIO
Yes, Peter, to hide her face. Because her fan's
prettier to look at.

NURSE
Good morning, gentlemen.

MERCUTIO
Good afternoon, lady.

NURSE
Is it good den?

MERCUTIO
'Tis no less, I tell ye, for the bawdy hand of the dial is now upon the prick of noon.

NURSE
Out upon you, what a man are you?

ROMEO
One, gentlewoman, that God hath made, himself to mar.

NURSE
By my troth, it is well said; 'for himself to mar', quoth'a'? Gentlemen, can any of you tell me where I may find the young Romeo?

ROMEO
I can tell you, but young Romeo will be older when you have found him than he was when you sought him: I am the youngest of that name, for fault of a worse.

NURSE
You say well.

MERCUTIO
Yea, is the worst well? Very well took, i'faith, wisely, wisely.

NURSE
If you be he, sir, I desire some confidence with you.

BENVOLIO
She will indite him to some supper.

MERCUTIO
A bawd, a bawd, a bawd! So ho!

NURSE
Is it the afternoon?

MERCUTIO
Not far off. Because the
clock is just about to strike twelve.

NURSE
Oh, go away! Who on earth are you?

ROMEO
Someone, Madam, that God made to spite
himself.

NURSE
Goodness me, that's well said – 'to spite himself'
did you say? Gentlemen, can any of you tell me where I
might find young Romeo?

ROMEO
I can tell you but 'young' Romeo will be older by the time
you find him than he was when you first looked for him.
I'm the youngest with that name, unless you know another.

NURSE
Very well said.

MERCUTIO
Was that well said? Well taken, I'll admit.
Yes, very.

NURSE
If you are him, sir, I would like to speak with
you.

BENVOLIO
She's going to ask him to supper.

MERCUTIO
Quite the madam! Ho ho!

ROMEO
What hast thou found?

MERCUTIO
No hare, sir, unless a hare, sir, in a lenten pie,
that is something stale and hoar ere it be spent.

Sings

An old hare hoar,
And an old hare hoar,
Is very good meat in lent;
But a hare that is hoar
Is too much for a score,
When it hoars ere it be spent.

Romeo, will you come to your father's? We'll
to dinner, thither.

ROMEO
I will follow you.

MERCUTIO
Farewell, ancient lady, farewell,

Singing

'lady, lady.'

Exeunt MERCUTIO and BENVOLIO

NURSE
I pray you, sir, what saucy
merchant was this, that was so full of his ropery?

ROMEO
A gentleman, Nurse, that loves to hear himself talk,
and will speak more in a minute than he will stand
to in a month.

ROMEO
What did you say?

MERCUTIO
Nothing. Or nothing that you'd want to hear.
It's old and meaningless before you've even heard it.

Sings

Something that is old,
Yes, something that is old,
Is better than nothing at all.
But an old thing
Is something no-one's wanting
When it's old before used at all.

Romeo, will you come to your father's? We're having dinner there.

ROMEO
I'll come in a bit.

MERCUTIO
Goodbye, old lady. Goodbye,

Singing

'Lady, lady.'

Exeunt MERCUTIO and BENVOLIO

NURSE
Please, sir, who was that rude
man that was so full of himself?

ROMEO
Someone, Nurse, that loves to hear himself talk
and will say more in a minute than he will listen
to in a month.

NURSE
An 'a speak any thing against me, I'll take him down,
an 'a were lustier than he is, and twenty such
Jacks; and if I cannot, I'll find those that shall.
Scurvy knave, I am none of his flirt-gills, I am
none of his skains-mates. And thou must stand by too
and suffer every knave to use me at his pleasure!

PETER
I saw no man use you a pleasure; if I had, my
weapon should quickly have been out. I warrant you,
I dare draw as soon as another man, if I see occasion in a
good quarrel, and the law on my side.

NURSE
Now, afore God, I am so vexed that every part about
me quivers. Scurvy knave! Pray you, sir, a word:
and as I told you, my young lady bade me enquire you
out; what she bade me say, I will keep to myself.
But first let me tell ye, if ye should lead her in
a fool's paradise, as they say, it were a very gross
kind of behaviour, as they say; for the gentlewoman
is young; and therefore, if you should deal double
with her, truly it were an ill thing to be offered
to any gentlewoman, and very weak dealing.

ROMEO
Nurse, commend me to thy lady and mistress. I
protest unto thee -

NURSE
Good heart, and, i'faith, I will tell her as much:
Lord, Lord, she will be a joyful woman.

ROMEO
What wilt thou tell her, Nurse? thou dost not mark me.

NURSE
I will tell her, sir, that you do protest, which, as
I take it, is a gentleman-like offer.

NURSE
If he says anything else against me, I'll have him -
even if he had more energy and there were twenty
of him. And, if I couldn't, I'd find someone who could.
Rude man! I'm not one of those flirty girls! I'm
not one of his conquests! And you just stood there
and let him use me however he wanted?

PETER
I don't think he used you how he wanted. If he had, I
would have drawn my sword, believe me.
I'm as ready to fight as any another man, if there's reason
for it and it's legal.

NURSE
Good God! I am so wound up that every part of
me is trembling. Rude man! Now, sir, might I have a word.
As I said, a young lady asked me to find you
What she asked me to say I will keep to myself.
But first let me tell you - if you should lead her on
a fool's errand, as they say, it would be very bad
form, as they say, because the woman
is young. And therefore, if you were *to* mislead
her, it would be a very improper thing to do
to any woman, and would be very poor behaviour.

ROMEO
Nurse, send my love to Juliet. And I
promise you…

NURSE
You won't. And, I promise, I'll tell her that.
Good Lord, she will be very happy.

ROMEO
What will you tell her, Nurse? You didn't let me finish.

NURSE
I will tell her, sir, that you do promise. Which,
I believe, was done with utmost sincerity.

ROMEO
Bid her devise
Some means to come to shrift this afternoon,
And there she shall at Friar Lawrence' cell
Be shrived and married. Here is for thy pains.

NURSE
No truly, sir, not a penny.

ROMEO
Go to, I say you shall.

NURSE
This afternoon, sir? Well, she shall be there.

ROMEO
And stay, good Nurse, behind the abbey wall:
Within this hour my man shall be with thee,
And bring thee cords made like a tackled stair,
Which to the high top-gallant of my joy
Must be my convoy in the secret night.
Farewell, be trusty, and I'll quit thy pains.
Farewell, commend me to thy mistress.

NURSE
Now God in heaven bless thee! Hark you, sir.

ROMEO
What say'st thou, my dear Nurse?

NURSE
Is your man secret? Did you ne'er hear say,
Two may keep counsel, putting one away?

ROMEO
'Warrant thee, my man's as true as steel.

ROMEO
Tell her to find
Some way to come to confession this afternoon
And there, at Friar Lawrence's church, she will
Be absolved and married. This is for you.

NURSE
No, honestly, sir - I won't take a penny.

ROMEO
Nonsense – I insist.

NURSE
This afternoon, sir? She'll be there.

ROMEO
Wait, Nurse, behind the abbey wall.
Within the hour my friend will come to you
And bring you some rope made into a ladder
Which will help me to get to her bedroom
And will be my way in tonight.
Goodbye. Stay true and I'll reimburse you for your trouble
Goodbye. Send my love to Juliet.

NURSE
God bless you! Wait, sir!

ROMEO
What is it, Nurse?

NURSE
Is your friend trustworthy? Have you heard the expression,
Two can plot together to betray another?

ROMEO
I promise you - my friend's very reliable.

NURSE
Well, sir, my mistress is the sweetest lady - Lord,
Lord! when 'twas a little prating thing - O, there
is a nobleman in town, one Paris, that would fain
lay knife aboard; but she, good soul, had as lieve
see a toad, a very toad, as see him. I anger her
sometimes, and tell her that Paris is the properer
man, but I'll warrant you, when I say so, she looks
as pale as any clout in the versal world. Doth not
rosemary and Romeo begin both with a letter?

ROMEO
Ay, Nurse, what of that? Both with an R.

NURSE
Ah, mocker, that's the dog-name; R is for
the – no, I know it begins with some other
letter - and she hath the prettiest sententious of
it, of you and rosemary, that it would do you good
to hear it.

ROMEO
Commend me to thy lady.

NURSE
Ay, a thousand times.

Exit Romeo

Peter!

PETER
Anon.

NURSE
Before and apace.

Exeunt

NURSE
That's good. Juliet is the sweetest lady ever. Good Lord! Since she was just a tiny little thing… Oh, there is a rich man in town, called Paris, that wants to claim Juliet as his own. But she, bless her, would rather date a toad, yes - a toad, than date him. I annoy her sometimes and tell her that Paris is the better man but, I promise you, when I say so she looks as white as any sheet in the whole world. Don't rosemary and Romeo begin with the same letter?

ROMEO
Yes, nurse. But so what? Both begin with an R.

NURSE
Ah, tease! That's the sound a dog makes. R is for… No, I'm thinking of a different letter. And she was the one who thought of it - of you and rosemary starting the same, I wish you could hear what she says about you.

ROMEO
Send her my love.

NURSE
I will do. A thousand times.

Exit Romeo

Peter!

PETER
Yes!

NURSE
Let's go. Quickly.

Exeunt

ACT II SCENE V. Capulet's orchard.

Enter JULIET

JULIET
The clock struck nine when I did send the Nurse;
In half an hour she promised to return.
Perchance she cannot meet him: that's not so.
O, she is lame! Love's heralds should be thoughts,
Which ten times faster glide than the sun's beams,
Driving back shadows over louring hills:
Therefore do nimble-pinioned doves draw Love,
And therefore hath the wind-swift Cupid wings.
Now is the sun upon the highmost hill
Of this day's journey, and from nine till twelve
Is three long hours, yet she is not come.
Had she affections and warm youthful blood,
She would be as swift in motion as a ball;
My words would bandy her to my sweet love,
And his to me.
But old folks, many feign as they were dead,
Unwieldy, slow, heavy, and pale as lead.
O God, she comes!

Enter Nurse and PETER

O honey Nurse, what news?
Hast thou met with him? Send thy man away.

NURSE
Peter, stay at the gate.

Exit PETER

JULIET
Now, good sweet Nurse - O Lord, why look'st thou sad?
Though news be sad, yet tell them merrily;
If good, thou shamest the music of sweet news
By playing it to me with so sour a face.

NURSE
I am a-weary, give me leave awhile.
Fie, how my bones ache! What a jaunce have I!

ACT II SCENE V. Capulet's orchard.

Enter JULIET

JULIET
It had just gone nine when I sent the nurse out.
She promised to return in half an hour.
Maybe she couldn't find him. No, that can't be it.
Oh, she's useless! Love should be conveyed by thought,
Which is ten times faster than the sunlight,
That forces shadows back over hills.
That's why love needs to have the wings of a dove
And why Cupid has wings.
Now the sun is at the highest point
That it reaches during the day and from nine till twelve
Is three long hours and yet she's still not come back.
If she felt how I do, and was young and vibrant,
She would be quicker about her task.
My words would carry her to my love
And his send her back to me.
But many old people act as if they were dead -
Unsteady, slow, lumbering and deathly pale.
Oh good, here she comes now!

Enter Nurse and PETER

Oh, darling Nurse, what do you have to tell me?
Did you speak to him? Tell your servant to go away.

NURSE
Peter, go and wait by the gate.

Exit PETER

JULIET
Now please, darling Nurse... Oh God, why are you so sad?
If your news is sad, say it happily.
If it's good, then you're doing it a disservice
By giving it to me with such a serious face.

NURSE
I'm tired. Give me a moment.
Oh, my limbs ache so much! I've had such a trek!

JULIET
I would thou hadst my bones, and I thy news.
Nay, come, I pray thee speak, good, good Nurse, speak.

NURSE
Jesu, what haste! can you not stay a while?
Do you not see that I am out of breath?

JULIET
How art thou out of breath, when thou hast breath
To say to me that thou art out of breath?
The excuse that thou dost make in this delay
Is longer than the tale thou dost excuse.
Is thy news good, or bad? Answer to that;
Say either, and I'll stay the circumstance:
Let me be satisfied, is't good or bad?

NURSE
Well, you have made a simple choice, you know not
how to choose a man: Romeo? no, not he; though his
face be better than any man's, yet his leg excels
all men's, and for a hand and a foot and a body,
though they be not to be talked on, yet they are
past compare. He is not the flower of courtesy,
but, I'll warrant him, as gentle as a lamb. Go thy
ways, wench, serve God. What, have you dined at home?

JULIET
No, no! But all this did I know before.
What says he of our marriage, what of that?

NURSE
Lord, how my head aches! what a head have I!
It beats as it would fall in twenty pieces.
My back a't'other side - ah, my back, my back!
Beshrew your heart for sending me about
To catch my death with jauncing up and down!

JULIET
I'faith, I am sorry that thou art not well.
Sweet, sweet, sweet Nurse, tell me, what says my love?

JULIET
I wish you had my limbs and I had your news.
Now, come on - please tell me, darling Nurse. Tell me.

NURSE
God, what's the rush? Can't you wait a bit?
Can't you see I'm out of breath?

JULIET
How can you be out of breath when you have enough
To say that you are out of breath?
The excuse that you're making to delay
Is taking longer than the news you're avoiding telling me.
Is your news good or bad? Tell me that.
Whichever you say, I'll prepare myself.
At least tell me that - is it good or bad?

NURSE
Well, you've made a foolish choice. You don't know
how to choose a man. Romeo? No, not him. Though his
face is better looking than any other's. And his legs better
than other's. And his hands, and his feet, and his body -
though I shouldn't talk about them - they are
beyond compare. He is not the most courteous
but, I'll admit that he's very civil. Go on
now, girl - to your duties. Have you eaten?

JULIET
No, no. But I knew all this before.
What did he say about marriage? What about that?

NURSE
Goodness, my head hurts! I've got such a bad headache!
It beats so hard it's like it's about to break into pieces.
And my back as well. Oh, my back, my back!
Shame on you for sending me out
To catch my death with all this traipsing up and down!

JULIET
I swear I'm sorry that you don't feel well.
Please, please, please, Nurse, tell me - what did he say?

NURSE
Your love says, like an honest gentleman, And a courteous, and a kind, and a handsome, And I warrant a virtuous - Where is your mother?

JULIET
Where is my mother? why, she is within,
Where should she be? How oddly thou repliest:
'Your love says, like an honest gentleman,
"Where is your mother?"'

NURSE
O God's lady dear,
Are you so hot? Marry come up, I trow;
Is this the poultice for my aching bones?
Henceforward do your messages yourself.

JULIET
Here's such a coil! Come, what says Romeo?

NURSE
Have you got leave to go to shrift today?

JULIET
I have.

NURSE
Then hie you hence to Friar Lawrence' cell,
There stays a husband to make you a wife.
Now comes the wanton blood up in your cheeks,
They'll be in scarlet straight at any news.
Hie you to church, I must another way,
To fetch a ladder, by the which your love
Must climb a bird's nest soon when it is dark.
I am the drudge, and toil in your delight;
But you shall bear the burden soon at night.
Go, I'll to dinner, hie you to the cell.

JULIET
Hie to high fortune! Honest Nurse, farewell.

Exeunt

NURSE
He said, like an honest man, and a
polite, and a kind, and a handsome, and, I'll
bet, a respectful... Where is your mother?

JULIET
Where is my mother? Why, she's indoors.
Where else would she be? What an odd thing to say!
He said, like an honest man,
Where is your mother?'

NURSE
Oh for God's sake!
Why are you so worked up? God give me strength.
Is this the best you can do to soothe my aching bones?
From now on you can take your messages yourself.

JULIET
What a fuss! Come on, what did Romeo say?

NURSE
Have you got permission to go to confession today?

JULIET
I have.

NURSE
Then go to Friar Lawrence's church.
There you'll find a man who wants to make you his wife.
That's put some colour in your cheeks -
They've gone bright red on hearing that.
Get to the church. I've got to find some way
Of getting a ladder by which Romeo
Will climb into your bedroom when it is dark.
I am a slave working for your enjoyment
But you'll be the one doing the work tonight.
Go on. I'll go to dinner. Get to the church.

JULIET
I go to my destiny! Goodbye, darling Nurse.

Exeunt

ACT II SCENE VI. Friar Lawrence's cell.

Enter FRIAR LAWRENCE and ROMEO

FRIAR LAWRENCE
So smile the heavens upon this holy act,
That after-hours with sorrow chide us not.

ROMEO
Amen, amen! but come what sorrow can,
It cannot countervail the exchange of joy
That one short minute gives me in her sight.
Do thou but close our hands with holy words,
Then love-devouring Death do what he dare,
It is enough I may but call her mine.

FRIAR LAWRENCE
These violent delights have violent ends,
And in their triumph die like fire and powder,
Which as they kiss consume. The sweetest honey
Is loathsome in his own deliciousness,
And in the taste confounds the appetite.
Therefore love moderately, long love doth so;
Too swift arrives as tardy as too slow.

Enter JULIET

Here comes the lady. O, so light a foot
Will ne'er wear out the everlasting flint;
A lover may bestride the gossamers
That idles in the wanton summer air,
And yet not fall, so light is vanity.

JULIET
Good even to my ghostly confessor.

FRIAR LAWRENCE
Romeo shall thank thee, daughter, for us both.

JULIET
As much to him, else is his thanks too much.

ACT II SCENE VI. Friar Lawrence's cell.

Enter FRIAR LAWRENCE and ROMEO

FRIAR LAWRENCE
The heavens smile upon us for doing this.
And even afterwards we won't regret it.

ROMEO
Amen to that! But whatever regrets there may be
Cannot outweigh this feeling of joy
That I get from seeing her just for a minute.
If you will join us in holy matrimony
Then I won't care what terrible things happen afterwards.
It will be enough that I will be able to say she's my wife.

FRIAR LAWRENCE
Such fierce emotions often lead to fierce consequences
And even at their peak crash and burn -
Destroyed by their own passion. The sweetest things
Can soon taste bitter once you have them
And make you regret wanting them.
So I'd say be patient in your love to make it last longer.
You'll still get the same benefits.

Enter JULIET

Here she comes. Such a graceful lady.
She'll never cause you to fall out of love.
Someone in love feels like they could walk on a cobweb
That's floating in the summer air,
And not fall off. It gives them such a light feeling.

JULIET
Good evening. Friar Lawrence.

FRIAR LAWRENCE
Romeo will greet you, my child, for us both.

JULIET
I'll do the same to him, or his greeting'll seem too much.

ROMEO
Ah, Juliet, if the measure of thy joy
Be heaped like mine and that thy skill be more
To blazon it, then sweeten with thy breath
This neighbour air, and let rich music's tongue
Unfold the imagined happiness that both
Receive in either by this dear encounter.

JULIET
Conceit, more rich in matter than in words,
Brags of his substance, not of ornament;
They are but beggars that can count their worth,
But my true love is grown to such excess
I cannot sum up sum of half my wealth.

FRIAR LAWRENCE
Come, come with me, and we will make short work,
For by your leaves, you shall not stay alone
Till Holy Church incorporate two in one.

Exeunt

ROMEO
Ah, Juliet, if the joy that you feel
Is as great as mine and you are more able
To express it, then use your sweet breath
To say it and let your words
Tell the hidden happiness we both
Feel on seeing each other.

JULIET
How I feel cannot be adequately expressed in words.
It's the feeling that's important - not the description.
It would make it seem less if I tried to express it
And my love has grown so much that
I could not even describe half of what I feel.

FRIAR LAWRENCE
Come on - come with me and we'll soon be done
Because, forgive me, but you mustn't be left alone
Until you have been made husband and wife.

Exeunt

ACT III SCENE I. A public place.

Enter MERCUTIO, BENVOLIO, Page, and Servants

BENVOLIO
I pray thee, good Mercutio, let's retire:
The day is hot, the Capulets abroad,
And, if we meet, we shall not scape a brawl,
For now, these hot days, is the mad blood stirring.

MERCUTIO
Thou art like one of those fellows, that when he
enters the confines of a tavern, claps me his sword
upon the table, and says 'God send me no need of
thee!'; and by the operation of the second cup draws
it on the drawer, when indeed there is no need.

BENVOLIO
Am I like such a fellow?

MERCUTIO
Come, come, thou art as hot a Jack in thy mood as
any in Italy, and as soon moved to be moody, and as
soon moody to be moved.

BENVOLIO
And what to?

MERCUTIO
Nay, an there were two such, we should have none
shortly, for one would kill the other. Thou? why,
thou wilt quarrel with a man that hath a hair more
or a hair less in his beard, than thou hast; thou
wilt quarrel with a man for cracking nuts, having no
other reason but because thou hast hazel eyes. What
eye but such an eye would spy out such a quarrel?
Thy head is as fun of quarrels as an egg is full of
meat, and yet thy head hath been beaten as addle as
an egg for quarrelling. Thou hast quarrelled with a
man for coughing in the street, because he hath
wakened thy dog that hath lain asleep in the sun.
Didst thou not fall out with a tailor for wearing
his new doublet before Easter? with another, for
tying his new shoes with old riband? and yet thou
wilt tutor me from quarrelling?

ACT III SCENE I. A public place.

Enter MERCUTIO, BENVOLIO, Page, and Servants

BENVOLIO
Please, Mercutio, let's go home.
It's hot today. The Capulets are nearby
And if we meet them we'll end up fighting them.
Because hot days lead to hot-bloodedness.

MERCUTIO
You're just like one of those people that, when he
enters the bar of a tavern, puts his sword
on the table and says 'I hope I won't have to use
this!' but after his second drink draws
his weapon on the barman when there wasn't any need.

BENVOLIO
Am I really like that?

MERCUTIO
Come on! You're as hot-blooded as
any man in Italy. And as soon provoked to be angered as
you would be angry to be provoked.

BENVOLIO
You what?

MERCUTIO
If there were two men like you we'd soon have
none because one would kill the other. You, yes,
you, would pick a fight with a man who had one hair more,
or one hair less, in his beard than you. You
would pick a fight with a man for cracking nuts, having no
other reason than because you have hazel eyes. What
other man would look to fight over something like that?
In your mind you're always looking for a
fight and yet you've been beaten soundly
for starting a fight. You have fought with a
man for coughing in the street because he
woke your dog that was lying in the sun.
Didn't you fall out with a tailor for wearing
his new jacket before Easter? With another for
tying his new shoes with old laces? And yet you
lecture me about fighting!

BENVOLIO
An I were so apt to quarrel as thou art, any man
should buy the fee-simple of my life for an hour and a quarter.

MERCUTIO
The fee-simple? O simple!

BENVOLIO
By my head, here comes the Capulets.

MERCUTIO
By my heel, I care not.

Enter TYBALT and others

TYBALT
Follow me close, for I will speak to them.
Gentlemen, good den, a word with one of you.

MERCUTIO
And but one word with one of us? couple it with
something; make it a word and a blow.

TYBALT
You shall find me apt enough to that, sir, and you
will give me occasion.

MERCUTIO
Could you not take some occasion without giving?

TYBALT
Mercutio, thou consortest with Romeo.

MERCUTIO
Consort? what, dost thou make us minstrels? And
thou make minstrels of us, look to hear nothing but
discords. Here's my fiddlestick, here's that shall
make you dance. 'Zounds, consort!

BENVOLIO
We talk here in the public haunt of men:
Either withdraw unto some private place,
And reason coldly of your grievances,
Or else depart; here all eyes gaze on us.

BENVOLIO
And, if I were as willing to fight as you are, any man
would make me pay for it with my life in an hour and a quarter.

MERCUTIO
With your life! Oh good lord!

BENVOLIO
Look out - here come the Capulets.

MERCUTIO
So what? I don't care.

Enter TYBALT and others

TYBALT
Stay close to me - I will speak to them.
Hello, gentlemen. Might I have a word with one of you?

MERCUTIO
You want just one word with one of us? Make it more
than that - make it a word and a *blow*.

TYBALT
You'll find I'm more than ready for that, sir, if you
give me a reason.

MERCUTIO
Couldn't you find a reason without me giving it to you?

TYBALT
Mercutio, you've been seen with Romeo…

MERCUTIO
Been seen? What are you implying? If
you're making fun of us, you'll regret
it. I have my sword with me and I'm ready
to take you on. Good God! Seen with?

BENVOLIO
We're in a public place.
Either go somewhere quieter
Or talk it over calmly.
Otherwise leave - everyone's looking at us.

MERCUTIO
Men's eyes were made to look, and let them gaze;
I will not budge for no man's pleasure, I.

Enter ROMEO

TYBALT
Well, peace be with you, sir, here comes my man.

MERCUTIO
But I'll be hanged, sir, if he wear your livery:
Marry, go before to field, he'll be your follower;
Your worship in that sense may call him man.

TYBALT
Romeo, the love I bear thee can afford
No better term than this: thou art a villain.

ROMEO
Tybalt, the reason that I have to love thee
Doth much excuse the appertaining rage
To such a greeting. Villain am I none;
Therefore farewell, I see thou knowest me not.

TYBALT
Boy, this shall not excuse the injuries
That thou hast done me, therefore turn and draw.

ROMEO
I do protest I never injured thee,
But love thee better than thou canst devise,
Till thou shalt know the reason of my love;
And so, good Capulet, which name I tender
As dearly as my own, be satisfied.

MERCUTIO
O calm, dishonourable, vile submission!
'Alla stoccata' carries it away.

Draws

Tybalt, you rat-catcher, will you walk?

TYBALT
What wouldst thou have with me?

MERCUTIO
That's what people do. Let them look -
I'm not going anywhere.

Enter ROMEO

TYBALT
Whatever. Here comes the man I want to see.

MERCUTIO
But I will die, sir, before I let you have him.
If you were to go to war, he'd be right behind.
He'd soon make you realise he is a man.

TYBALT
Romeo, how I feel about you means I cannot
Speak any higher of you than this - you are a bad man.

ROMEO
Tybalt, the way I feel towards you now
Makes me overlook how I would normally react
To such a comment. I am not a bad man
And so I'll say goodbye. I see you don't really know me.

TYBALT
Oi, this doesn't make up for the insult
That you did to me. Come back and draw your sword.

ROMEO
I swear I never insulted you.
I love you more than you can possibly know
Until you know the reason why this is so.
And so, Tybalt - who I care about
As much as I do about myself - I hope that satisfies you.

MERCUTIO
How calmly, cowardly, horribly you gave in!
I'll soon settle this.

Draws

Tybalt, you beast, will you fight me?

TYBALT
What do you want with me?

MERCUTIO
Good King of Cats, nothing but one of your nine
lives that I mean to make bold withal, and as you
shall use me hereafter, dry-beat the rest of the
eight. Will you pluck your sword out of his pilcher
by the ears? Make haste, lest mine be about your
ears ere it be out.

TYBALT
I am for you.

Drawing

ROMEO
Gentle Mercutio, put thy rapier up.

MERCUTIO
Come, sir, your 'passado'.

They fight

ROMEO
Draw, Benvolio, beat down their weapons.
Gentlemen, for shame forbear this outrage!
Tybalt, Mercutio, the prince expressly hath
Forbid bandying in Verona streets.
Hold, Tybalt! Good Mercutio!

TYBALT under ROMEO's arm stabs MERCUTIO, and flies with his followers

MERCUTIO
I am hurt.
A plague a'both houses! I am sped.
Is he gone and hath nothing?

BENVOLIO
What, art thou hurt?

MERCUTIO
Ay, ay, a scratch, a scratch, marry, 'tis enough.
Where is my page? Go, villain, fetch a surgeon.

Exit Page

ROMEO
Courage, man, the hurt cannot be much.

MERCUTIO
Nothing, Mr Cat-ulet, except your
life - which I intend to take shortly. If you
face me now, I'll soon beat it out of
you. Will you draw your sword from its scabbard
by the hilt? Quickly now, or mine will be at your
throat before you have a chance.

TYBALT
I'll take you on.

Drawing

ROMEO
Please, Mercutio, put your sword away.

MERCUTIO
Come on then, you. Fight!

They fight

ROMEO
Get out your sword, Benvolio, and stop them fighting.
Gentlemen, for pity's sake, stop this!
Tybalt, Mercutio, the Prince has expressly
Forbidden fighting in the streets of Verona.
Stop, Tybalt! Please, Mercutio!

TYBALT under ROMEO's arm stabs MERCUTIO, and flies with his followers

MERCUTIO
I've been hit.
To hell with the lot of you! I've been killed.
Has he gone? And missed his victory?

BENVOLIO
Have you been hurt?

MERCUTIO
Yes, yes - it's just a scratch, a scratch - but it's enough.
Where is my servant? Go, you idiot, get a doctor.

Exit Page

ROMEO
Come on. It can't be that bad.

MERCUTIO
No, 'tis not so deep as a well, nor so wide as a
church-door, but 'tis enough, 'twill serve. Ask for
me tomorrow, and you shall find me a grave man. I
am peppered, I warrant, for this world. A plague
a'both your houses! 'Zounds, a dog, a rat, a mouse, a
cat, to scratch a man to death! a braggart, a
rogue, a villain, that fights by the book of
arithmetic! Why the dev'l came you between us? I
was hurt under your arm.

ROMEO
I thought all for the best.

MERCUTIO
Help me into some house, Benvolio,
Or I shall faint. A plague a'both your houses!
They have made worms' meat of me. I have it,
And soundly too. Your houses!

Exeunt MERCUTIO and BENVOLIO

ROMEO
This gentleman, the Prince's near ally,
My very friend, hath got his mortal hurt
In my behalf; my reputation stain'd
With Tybalt's slander - Tybalt, that an hour
Hath been my cousin. O sweet Juliet,
Thy beauty hath made me effeminate,
And in my temper softened valour's steel!

Re-enter BENVOLIO

BENVOLIO
O Romeo, Romeo, brave Mercutio is dead!
That gallant spirit hath aspired the clouds,
Which too untimely here did scorn the earth.

ROMEO
This day's black fate on moe days doth depend,
This but begins the woe others must end.

Re-enter TYBALT

MERCUTIO
True - it's not as deep as a well nor as wide as a
church door. But it's enough - it will do. If you ask for
me tomorrow, you will find me in a grave. I
am done for, at least, in this life. To hell with
the lot of you! God, even a dog, a rat, a mouse, a
cat, could scratch a man to death! But a show-off, a
thug, a crook, who fights so
properly? Why on earth did you interfere? He
stabbed me under your arm.

ROMEO
I thought it was for the best.

MERCUTIO
Help me to a house, Benvolio,
Or I will pass out. To hell with the lot of you!
They have carved me up good and proper - I know it.
And it's been well done too. Damn you!

Exeunt MERCUTIO and BENVOLIO

ROMEO
This man, the Prince's close friend,
My good friend, has been hurt
Because of me. My reputation was tarnished
With Tybalt's words. Tybalt - that for an hour
Has been part of my family! Oh, dear Juliet,
Your beauty has made me weak
And that made me reluctant to fight!

Re-enter BENVOLIO

BENVOLIO
Oh, Romeo, Romeo - poor Mercutio's dead!
His brave spirit has gone to heaven,
His time here on earth was far too short.

ROMEO
The consequences of today's actions will become clear.
This is just the start of the trouble that others will face.

Re-enter TYBALT

BENVOLIO
Here comes the furious Tybalt back again.

ROMEO
Again, in triumph, and Mercutio slain!
Away to heaven, respective lenity,
And fire-eyed fury be my conduct now!
Now, Tybalt, take the 'villain' back again,
That late thou gavest me, for Mercutio's soul
Is but a little way above our heads,
Staying for thine to keep him company:
Either thou or I, or both, must go with him.

TYBALT
Thou wretched boy, that didst consort him here,
Shalt with him hence.

ROMEO
This shall determine that.

They fight; TYBALT falls

BENVOLIO
Romeo, away, be gone!
The citizens are up, and Tybalt slain.
Stand not amazed, the Prince will doom thee death,
If thou art taken. Hence be gone, away!

ROMEO
O, I am fortune's fool!

BENVOLIO
Why dost thou stay?

Exit ROMEO

Enter Citizens, & c

First Citizen
Which way ran he that killed Mercutio?
Tybalt, that murderer, which way ran he?

BENVOLIO
Tybalt's back again.

ROMEO
Again? To crow over Mercutio death!
To hell with staying calm and respectable.
My anger will control me now!
Now, Tybalt, take back that slur
That you made against me. For Mercutio's ghost
Is hovering above our heads
Waiting for yours to keep it company.
Either you, or I, or both, will go with him.

TYBALT
You wicked boy. You brought him here.
And you will leave with him.

ROMEO
We'll soon see about that.

They fight; TYBALT falls

BENVOLIO
Romeo, go, go on!
The citizens have woken up and Tybalt is dead.
Don't stand there staring - the Prince will have you killed
If you're caught. Quick – go, now!

ROMEO
Oh, I am the victim of fate!

BENVOLIO
What are you waiting for?

Exit ROMEO

Enter Citizens, & c

First Citizen
Which way did the man who killed Mercutio go?
Tybalt - the murderer - which way did he go?

BENVOLIO
There lies that Tybalt.

First Citizen
Up, sir, go with me;
I charge thee in the Prince's name obey.

Enter Prince, attended; MONTAGUE, CAPULET, their Wives, and others

PRINCE
Where are the vile beginners of this fray?

BENVOLIO
O noble prince, I can discover all
The unlucky manage of this fatal brawl;
There lies the man, slain by young Romeo,
That slew thy kinsman, brave Mercutio.

LADY CAPULET
Tybalt, my cousin! O my brother's child!
O Prince! O husband! O, the blood is spilled
O my dear kinsman. Prince, as thou art true,
For blood of ours, shed blood of Montague.
O cousin, cousin!

PRINCE
Benvolio, who began this bloody fray?

BENVOLIO
Tybalt, here slain, whom Romeo's hand did slay.
Romeo, that spoke him fair, bade him bethink
How nice the quarrel was, and urged withal
Your high displeasure; all this, uttered
With gentle breath, calm look, knees humbly bowed,
Could not take truce with the unruly spleen
Of Tybalt deaf to peace, but that he tilts
With piercing steel at bold Mercutio's breast,
Who, all as hot, turns deadly point to point,
And with a martial scorn, with one hand beats
Cold death aside, and with the other sends
It back to Tybalt, whose dexterity,
Retorts it. Romeo he cries aloud,

BENVOLIO
Tybalt's there.

First Citizen
Stand up, sir, you must come with me.
I order you, in the Prince's name, to obey me.

Enter Prince, attended; MONTAGUE, CAPULET, their Wives, and others

PRINCE
Where are the people who started this?

BENVOLIO
Prince, I can tell you everything
That happened in this terrible fight.
The man lying there, who was killed by Romeo,
Killed your relative - poor Mercutio.

LADY CAPULET
Tybalt! My nephew! Oh, my brother's son!
Oh, Prince! Oh, husband! The blood has been spilt
Of my dear nephew! Prince, if you meant what you said,
For killing one of our family, you must kill a Montague.
Oh, Tybalt, Tybalt!

PRINCE
Benvolio, who started this fight?

BENVOLIO
Tybalt, who's lies here dead - killed by Romeo.
Romeo tried to talk to him and make him think about
How petty their squabbling was and reminded him
About your warning. He said all this
In gentle tones, a calm expression and unthreatening pose
But he couldn't quell the uncontrollable temper
Of Tybalt who was deaf to talk of peace. And then he drew
His sword and pointed it at Mercutio's chest
Who was equally riled and drew his sword in turn
With a confident expression. With one hand he knocked
Tybalt's sword aside and with the other thrust
It back at Tybalt whose skill
Rebuffed it. Romeo called out,

'Hold, friends! friends, part!' and swifter than his tongue,
His agile arm beats down their fatal points,
And 'twixt them rushes; underneath whose arm
An envious thrust from Tybalt hit the life
Of stout Mercutio, and then Tybalt fled;
But by and by comes back to Romeo,
Who had but newly entertained revenge,
And to 't they go like lightning, for, ere I
Could draw to part them, was stout Tybalt slain;
And as he fell, did Romeo turn and fly.
This is the truth, or let Benvolio die.

LADY CAPULET
He is a kinsman to the Montague,
Affection makes him false, he speaks not true:
Some twenty of them fought in this black strife,
And all those twenty could but kill one life.
I beg for justice, which thou, Prince, must give:
Romeo slew Tybalt, Romeo must not live.

PRINCE
Romeo slew him, he slew Mercutio;
Who now the price of his dear blood doth owe?

MONTAGUE
Not Romeo, Prince, he was Mercutio's friend;
His fault concludes but what the law should end,
The life of Tybalt.

PRINCE
And for that offence
Immediately we do exile him hence.
I have an interest in your heart's proceeding:
My blood for your rude brawls doth lie a-bleeding;
But I'll amerce you with so strong a fine
That you shall all repent the loss of mine.
I will be deaf to pleading and excuses,
Nor tears nor prayers shall purchase out abuses:
Therefore use none. Let Romeo hence in haste,
Else, when he's found, that hour is his last.
Bear hence this body and attend our will:
Mercy but murders, pardoning those that kill.

Exeunt

'Stop, my friends! Friends, stop!' and, quicker than he spoke,
Tried to deflect their swords,
And dove between them. Underneath his arm
A vicious thrust from Tybalt took the life
Of Mercutio and then Tybalt fled.
But after a while he came back to Romeo,
Who by now had decided to seek revenge,
And they went at it like lightning. And, before I
Could attempt to stop them, Tybalt was killed.
And as he fell, Romeo turned and ran.
This is the truth, I swear on my life.

LADY CAPULET
He is a relative of the Montagues.
His loyalty makes him lie - he's not telling the truth.
At least twenty of them fought in this evil battle.
And yet they could only kill one person.
I demand justice, which you, Prince, must give.
Because Romeo killed Tybalt, Romeo must die.

PRINCE
Romeo killed him but he killed Mercutio.
Who should be made to pay for his death?

MONTAGUE
Not Romeo, Prince, he was Mercutio's friend.
He only did what the law would have done
And killed Tybalt.

PRINCE
And, for doing so,
He is henceforth banished from Verona.
I too have been affected by your feud -
Because of your fighting, my friend has been killed.
But I'll punish you with a fine so harsh
That you will regret any loss I have suffered.
I won't listen to pleading or excuses.
Neither tears nor begging will make me change my mind
So don't bother. Romeo must leave immediately.
If he is found, he will be put to death.
Take Tybalt's body away from here and do as I say.
Even mercy can be harsh when it pardons those that kill.

Exeunt

ACT III SCENE II. Capulet's orchard.

Enter JULIET

JULIET
Gallop apace, you fiery-footed steeds,
Towards Phoebus' lodging; such a waggoner
As Phaeton would whip you to the west,
And bring in cloudy night immediately.
Spread thy close curtain, love-performing Night,
That runaways' eyes may wink, and Romeo
Leap to these arms, untalked of and unseen:
Lovers can see to do their amorous rites
By their own beauties, or if love be blind,
It best agrees with night. Come, civil Night,
Thou sober-suited matron all in black,
And learn me how to lose a winning match,
Played for a pair of stainless maidenhoods.
Hood my unmanned blood, bating in my cheeks,
With thy black mantle, till strange love grow bold,
Think true love acted simple modesty.
Come, Night, come, Romeo, come, thou day in night,
For thou wilt lie upon the wings of night,
Whiter than new snow on a raven's back.
Come, gentle Night, come, loving, black-browed Night,
Give me my Romeo, and when I shall die,
Take him and cut him out in little stars,
And he will make the face of heaven so fine
That all the world will be in love with night
And pay no worship to the garish sun.
O, I have bought the mansion of a love,
But not possessed it, and though I am sold,
Not yet enjoyed. So tedious is this day
As is the night before some festival
To an impatient child that hath new robes
And may not wear them. O, here comes my Nurse,

Enter Nurse, with cords

And she brings news, and every tongue that speaks
But Romeo's name speaks heavenly eloquence.
Now, Nurse, what news? What hast thou there? the cords
That Romeo bid thee fetch?

ACT III SCENE II. Capulet's orchard.

Enter JULIET

JULIET
Why can't time go quicker?
Why can't the sun move across the sky faster?
Why is it taking so long to set?
I wish the night would come sooner
Swallowing everything up in its secretive darkness
So people are able to get away with things and Romeo
Can come to me without anyone seeing or noticing him.
Even at night, lovers can still see to do what they want
By being guided by their passion. Because love is blind
It best suits the night. Can't the night come sooner?
And cover everything in black.
Then I'll know what it's like to lose something but win
Because we'll both lose our virginity.
Be still my beating heart, that sends colour to my cheeks,
By staying calm until I can act on my new-found love.
My true feelings should be hidden by modesty.
I hope night comes soon and Romeo comes to light my life
Because, even thou he's coming at night,
He'll light it up as bright as anything.
Come on, night time, come on, lovely dark night,
Let Romeo come to me and, when I die,
I hope they make a picture of him in the stars
Because he would make the sky so bright
That everyone would want it to be night
And not be interested in the showy sun.
Oh, even though I am now married,
I have not yet consummated it. Although I am wedded,
I am not yet bedded. This day is taking so long -
Like the night before Christmas
For an impatient child that has new gifts
And can't yet enjoy them. Here comes the Nurse.

Enter Nurse, with cords

She must have news. And anyone who talks about
Romeo sounds wonderful.
Yes, Nurse, what is it? What do you have there? The ropes
That Romeo asked you to get?

NURSE
Ay, ay, the cords.

Throws them down

JULIET
Ay me, what news? Why dost thou wring thy hands?

NURSE
Ah weraday! he's dead, he's dead, he's dead!
We are undone, lady, we are undone.
Alack the day, he's gone, he's killed, he's dead!

JULIET
Can heaven be so envious?

NURSE
Romeo can,
Though heaven cannot. O Romeo, Romeo!
Who ever would have thought it? Romeo!

JULIET
What devil art thou, that dost torment me thus?
This torture should be roared in dismal hell.
Hath Romeo slain himself? Say thou but 'ay',
And that bare vowel 'I' shall poison more
Than the death-darting eye of cockatrice.
I am not I, if there be such an 'ay',
Or those eyes shut, that make thee answer 'ay'.
If he be slain, say 'ay', or if not, 'no':
Brief sounds determine of my weal or woe.

NURSE
I saw the wound, I saw it with mine eyes
God save the mark!, here on his manly breast:
A piteous corse, a bloody piteous corse,
Pale, pale as ashes, all bedaubed in blood,
All in gore-blood; I sounded at the sight.

JULIET
O break, my heart, poor bankrout, break at once!
To prison, eyes, ne'er look on liberty!
Vile earth, to earth resign, end motion here,
And thou and Romeo press one heavy bier!

NURSE
Yes, yes, the rope ladder.

Throws them down

JULIET
Goodness! What is it? Why are you wringing your hands?

NURSE
Oh, it's terrible! He's dead, he's dead, he's dead!
It's so terrible, Juliet, so terrible!
What a horrible day! He's gone, he's been killed, he's dead!

JULIET
Can God be so cruel?

NURSE
Romeo can.
Though God cannot. Oh, Romeo, Romeo!
Whoever would have thought it? Romeo!

JULIET
How can you be so cruel as to torture me like this?
Even the devil would object to this kind of treatment.
Has Romeo killed himself? If you say 'Yes',
Then that one word will hurt me more
Than the poisonous fangs of a snake.
I cannot live if it's possible that it's true.
But if he is dead that would make your answer 'Yes',
If he's dead, say 'yes'. Or if not, 'no'.
Such small words will determine if I am happy or sad.

NURSE
I saw the wound. I saw it with my own eyes -
God forbid! - here on his chest.
His poor body, his poor, bloody body.
Pale, pale as ash, all covered in blood,
Completely covered in blood. I fainted when I saw it.

JULIET
Oh, my heart is broken! Poor empty thing! Broken at once!
My eyes will never see anything as good!
Romeo will be buried and end his days under the earth.
The earth and Romeo will be one and the same!

NURSE
O Tybalt, Tybalt, the best friend I had!
O courteous Tybalt, honest gentleman,
That ever I should live to see thee dead!

JULIET
What storm is this that blows so contrary?
Is Romeo slaughtered? and is Tybalt dead?
My dearest cousin, and my dearer lord?
Then, dreadful trumpet, sound the general doom,
For who is living, if those two are gone?

NURSE
Tybalt is gone and Romeo banishéd,
Romeo that killed him, he is banishéd.

JULIET
O God, did Romeo's hand shed Tybalt's blood?

NURSE
It did, it did, alas the day, it did!

JULIET
O serpent heart, hid with a flow'ring face!
Did ever dragon keep so fair a cave?
Beautiful tyrant, fiend angelical!
Dove-feathered raven, wolvish-ravening lamb!
Despised substance of divinest show!
Just opposite to what thou justly seem'st,
A damnéd saint, an honourable villain!
O nature, what hadst thou to do in hell
When thou didst bower the spirit of a fiend
In mortal paradise of such sweet flesh?
Was ever book containing such vile matter
So fairly bound? O that deceit should dwell
In such a gorgeous palace!

NURSE
There's no trust,
No faith, no honesty in men, all perjured,
All forsworn, all naught, all dissemblers.
Ah, where's my man? Give me some aqua-vitae;
These griefs, these woes, these sorrows make me old.
Shame come to Romeo!

NURSE
Oh, Tybalt, Tybalt - the best friend I ever had!
Oh, darling Tybalt! Such an honest gentleman!
That I should ever live to see you dead!

JULIET
What terrible thing did you just say?
Is Romeo killed and Tybalt dead too?
My poor dear cousin and my dearest husband?
Then the world might as well end!
What's the point in living if those two are gone?

NURSE
Tybalt is dead and Romeo is banished.
Romeo killed him and has been banished.

JULIET
Oh, God! Romeo killed Tybalt?

NURSE
He did, he did. Regretfully, he did!

JULIET
Such an evil heart hidden by a beautiful face!
Was there ever something so bad in something so good?
He's a wonderful beast! A horrible angel!
An innocent criminal! A hideous delight!
A hated person with a beautiful face!
The opposite of what he seemed to be,
An evil saint, an honest crook!
Oh, God, how could it be
That the spirit of something so despicable
Could be found in such a gorgeous body?
Was there ever anything that contained so much evil
That looked so beautiful? Oh, how could wickedness exist
In such a handsome man!

NURSE
There's no reliability,
No goodness, no honesty, in men - they all lie,
All betray. They are all worthless, all crooks.
Where's my servant? Get me a drink.
This news, this sadness, this grief makes me feel old.
To hell with Romeo!

JULIET
Blistered be thy tongue
For such a wish! he was not born to shame:
Upon his brow shame is ashamed to sit;
For 'tis a throne where honour may be crowned
Sole monarch of the universal earth.
O what a beast was I to chide at him!

NURSE
Will you speak well of him that killed your cousin?

JULIET
Shall I speak ill of him that is my husband?
Ah, poor my lord, what tongue shall smooth thy name,
When I, thy three-hours wife, have mangled it?
But wherefore, villain, didst thou kill my cousin?
That villain cousin would have killed my husband:
Back, foolish tears, back to your native spring,
Your tributary drops belong to woe,
Which you mistaking offer up to joy.
My husband lives that Tybalt would have slain;
And Tybalt's dead that would have slain my husband:
All this is comfort, wherefore weep I then?
Some word there was, worser than Tybalt's death,
That murdered me; I would forget it fain,
But O, it presses to my memory,
Like damnéd guilty deeds to sinners' minds:
'Tybalt is dead, and Romeo--banishéd;'
That 'banishéd,' that one word 'banishéd,'
Hath slain ten thousand Tybalts. Tybalt's death
Was woe enough if it had ended there;
Or if sour woe delights in fellowship
And needly will be ranked with other griefs,
Why followed not, when she said 'Tybalt's dead',
'Thy father' or 'thy mother', nay, or both,
Which modern lamentation might have moved?
But with a rear-ward following Tybalt's death,
'Romeo is banishéd,' to speak that word,
Is father, mother, Tybalt, Romeo, Juliet,
All slain, all dead. 'Romeo is banishéd!'
There is no end, no limit, measure, bound,
In that word's death, no words can that woe sound.
Where is my father and my mother, Nurse?

JULIET
How dare you say
Something like that! He was not born this way.
He doesn't deserve to be cursed.
He is a very honourable man
And the only man in my whole world.
Oh, how could I have been so unkind about him!

NURSE
You'd speak up for the man that killed your cousin?

JULIET
Should I speak against the man that is my husband?
My poor husband. What can be done to clear your name,
When even I, your new wife, spoke against it?
But, why, you bad man, did you kill my cousin?
That evil cousin would have killed my husband.
No more crying. I won't have any more of it.
Crying is only right when I'm sad
And not now when I'm feeling happy.
My husband is alive though Tybalt would have killed him.
And Tybalt's dead who would have killed my husband.
This is good news. So why am I crying?
There's something else, worse than Tybalt's death,
That's affected me. I wish I could forget it
But it is stuck in my head -
Like guilty thoughts in sinners' minds.
'Tybalt is dead, and Romeo banished'
That word 'banished', that one word 'banished',
Is worse than ten thousand dead Tybalts. Tybalt's death
Was bad enough, if that had been all it was.
Or, if one misery must be followed by another
To be compared with other sorrows,
Why couldn't it be, after she said 'Tybalt's dead',
My father, or my mother, or even both -
Which might have been expected -
But instead following Tybalt's death,
'Romeo is banished'. To hear that word
Is as bad as if my father, mother, Tybalt, Romeo, Juliet,
Had all been killed – were all dead. 'Romeo is banished!'
There is nothing so final, so terrible, extreme, harsh,
As that one word. No words sound as bad as that.
Where are my father and my mother, Nurse?

NURSE
Weeping and wailing over Tybalt's corse.
Will you go to them? I will bring you thither.

JULIET
Wash they his wounds with tears? mine shall be spent,
When theirs are dry, for Romeo's banishment.
Take up those cords. Poor ropes, you are beguiled,
Both you and I, for Romeo is exiled.
He made you for a highway to my bed,
But I, a maid, die maiden-widowéd.
Come, cords, come, Nurse, I'll to my wedding bed;
And death, not Romeo, take my maidenhead!

NURSE
Hie to your chamber. I'll find Romeo
To comfort you, I wot well where he is.
Hark ye, your Romeo will be here at night.
I'll to him, he is hid at Lawrence' cell.

JULIET
O find him! Give this ring to my true knight,
And bid him come to take his last farewell.

Exeunt

NURSE
Crying over Tybalt's body.
Do you want to go to them? I will take you there.

JULIET
They're crying over his death. I'll still be crying,
Even when they've finished, over Romeo's banishment.
Bring up the ladder. Poor thing, it's been cheated -
Both it and I - because Romeo is banished.
He made you as a way to get to my bedroom
But I, a virgin, will die a virgin.
Come on, Nurse, bring the ladder up. I'll go to bed
And death, not Romeo, will take me to heaven!

NURSE
Go to your room. I'll find Romeo
To comfort you. I know where he is.
Listen to me - Romeo will be here tonight.
I'll go find him. He's hidden at Friar Lawrence's church.

JULIET
Oh, please find him! Give this ring to my dear husband
And ask him to come to say his goodbyes.

Exeunt

ACT III SCENE III. Friar Lawrence's cell.

Enter FRIAR LAWRENCE

FRIAR LAWRENCE
Romeo, come forth, come forth, thou fearful man:
Affliction is enamoured of thy parts,
And thou art wedded to calamity.

Enter ROMEO

ROMEO
Father, what news? What is the Prince's doom?
What sorrow craves acquaintance at my hand,
That I yet know not?

FRIAR LAWRENCE
Too familiar
Is my dear son with such sour company!
I bring thee tidings of the Prince's doom.

ROMEO
What less than doomsday is the Prince's doom?

FRIAR LAWRENCE
A gentler judgement vanished from his lips:
Not body's death, but body's banishment.

ROMEO
Ha, banishment? be merciful, say 'death':
For exile hath more terror in his look,
Much more than death. Do not say 'banishment'!

FRIAR LAWRENCE
Hence from Verona art thou banishéd:
Be patient, for the world is broad and wide.

ROMEO
There is no world without Verona walls,
But purgatory, torture, hell itself:
Hence 'banishéd' is banished from the world,
And world's exile is death; then 'banishéd'
Is death mistermed. Calling death 'banishéd',
Thou cut'st my head off with a golden axe,
And smilest upon the stroke that murders me.

ACT III SCENE III. Friar Lawrence's cell.

Enter FRIAR LAWRENCE

FRIAR LAWRENCE
Romeo, come here. Come here, you poor man.
You are very troubled
And seem to be dogged by misfortune.

Enter ROMEO

ROMEO
Father, is there any news? What did the Prince say?
What fate is to befall me
That I don't yet know about?

FRIAR LAWRENCE
Too often
Have you been faced with such sad news.
I've come to tell you the Prince's decision.

ROMEO
What else other than death can he have decided?

FRIAR LAWRENCE
That would have been kinder than what he said.
Not death, but banishment.

ROMEO
What? Banishment! Please no - say 'death'
Because banishment would be more terrible to me
Than death. Do not say 'banishment'.

FRIAR LAWRENCE
You have been banished from Verona.
But it's not too bad - there's a great wide world out there.

ROMEO
There is nowhere else in the world except Verona
Other than purgatory, damnation and hell itself.
So if I'm banished then I am banished to hell,
As being exiled from the world is to die. So banishment
Is another word for death. By calling death banishment
You might as well cut off my head with an axe
And think that what killed me was a blessing.

FRIAR LAWRENCE
O deadly sin! O rude unthankfulness!
Thy fault our law calls death, but the kind Prince,
Taking thy part, hath rushed aside the law,
And turned that black word 'death' to 'banishment':
This is dear mercy, and thou seest it not.

ROMEO
'Tis torture, and not mercy. Heaven is here
Where Juliet lives, and every cat and dog
And little mouse, every unworthy thing,
Live here in heaven, and may look on her,
But Romeo may not. More validity,
More honourable state, more courtship lives
In carrion-flies than Romeo; they my seize
On the white wonder of dear Juliet's hand,
And steal immortal blessing from her lips,
Who even in pure and vestal modesty
Still blush, as thinking their own kisses sin;
But Romeo may not, he is banishéd:
Flies may do this, but I from this must fly;
They are free men, but I am banishéd:
And sayest thou yet that exile is not death?
Hadst thou no poison mixed, no sharp-ground knife,
No sudden mean of death, though ne'er so mean,
But 'banishéd' to kill me? 'Banishéd'?
O Friar, the damnéd use that word in hell;
Howling attends it. How hast thou the heart,
Being a divine, a ghostly confessor,
A sin-absolver, and my friend professed,
To mangle me with that word 'banishéd'?

FRIAR LAWRENCE
Thou fond mad man, hear me a little speak.

ROMEO
O thou wilt speak again of banishment.

FRIAR LAWRENCE
I'll give thee armour to keep off that word:
Adversity's sweet milk, philosophy,
To comfort thee though thou art banishéd.

FRIAR LAWRENCE
Oh, how terrible! How ungrateful!
Your punishment should have been death but the Prince,
Taking your side, ignored the law
And changed the sentence from death to banishment.
This is merciful and yet you don't see it.

ROMEO
It's torture, not mercy. I want to be here
Where Juliet is. Every other living thing,
However small, however contemptible,
Can stay here with her and is allowed to look at her.
But I can't. It would be better,
More acceptable, more practical
If I were a fly than Romeo. Flies can touch
Her beautiful white hand
And steal kisses from her lips,
Who, in her pure and innocent shyness,
Would still blush as she thinks kisses are a sin.
But I can't. I've been banished.
Flies can do this but I have to fly from here.
They are free but I am banished.
And yet you say exile is better than death?
If you had any poison to hand, a sharp knife,
Any quick method of death, none would be as bad.
But banishment kills me. 'Banished'?
Oh, Friar, that is the worst word in the world.
It makes me want to scream. How can you,
Being so holy - a spiritual adviser,
A forgiver of sin, and my proven friend -
Bear to hurt me with that word 'banished'?

FRIAR LAWRENCE
You poor foolish man, listen to what I have to say.

ROMEO
You'll only talk more about banishment.

FRIAR LAWRENCE
I'll help you find a way to fight against that word -
The best remedy for trying times is reflection -
To comfort you even though you are banished.

ROMEO
Yet 'banishéd'? Hang up philosophy!
Unless philosophy can make a Juliet,
Displant a town, reverse a prince's doom,
It helps not, it prevails not; talk no more.

FRIAR LAWRENCE
O then I see that mad men have no ears.

ROMEO
How should they when that wise men have no eyes?

FRIAR LAWRENCE
Let me dispute with thee of thy estate.

ROMEO
Thou canst not speak of that thou dost not feel.
Wert thou as young as I, Juliet thy love,
An hour but married, Tybalt muderéd,
Doting like me, and like me banishéd,
Then mightst thou speak, then mightst thou tear thy hair,
And fall upon the ground as I do now,
Taking the measure of an unmade grave.

Knocking within

FRIAR LAWRENCE
Arise, one knocks. Good Romeo, hide thyself.

ROMEO
Not I, unless the breath of heart-sick groans,
Mist-like infold me from the search of eyes.

Knocking

FRIAR LAWRENCE
Hark, how they knock! - Who's there? - Romeo, arise,
Thou wilt be taken. - Stay a while! - Stand up;

Knocking

Run to my study. - By and by! - God's will,
What simpleness is this! - I come, I come!

ROMEO
Yes 'banished'. To hell with reflection!
Unless reflection can make another Juliet,
Relocate the town or undo the Prince's decision,
It doesn't help me. It won't help. So don't mention it.

FRIAR LAWRENCE
Oh, I see idiots aren't prepared to listen.

ROMEO
Why should they when wise men can't see clearly?

FRIAR LAWRENCE
Let me clarify what your situation is.

ROMEO
You can't talk about something you don't understand.
If you were as young as me, and Juliet was your wife,
You'd been married for an hour, and Tybalt murdered,
And you were as in love as me and like me banished,
Then you might know. Then you would tear out your hair,
And fall down on the ground - like I'm doing -
Measuring out the space for your grave.

Knocking within

FRIAR LAWRENCE
Get up. Someone's knocking. Please, Romeo, hide.

ROMEO
I won't. Not unless the sighs of my lovesick heart
Form a mist to conceal me from prying eyes.

Knocking

FRIAR LAWRENCE
Goodness, they're persistent! Who's there? Romeo, get up!
You'll be caught. - Just a minute! - Get up!

Knocking

Go to my room. - I'm coming! - Good God,
Why are you being so stupid! - I'm coming, I'm coming!

Knocking

Who knocks so hard? whence come you? what's your will?

NURSE
[Within] Let me come in, and you shall know
my errand:
I come from Lady Juliet.

FRIAR LAWRENCE
Welcome then.

Enter Nurse

NURSE
O holy Friar, O, tell me, holy Friar,
Where is my lady's lord, where's Romeo?

FRIAR LAWRENCE
There on the ground, with his own tears made drunk.

NURSE
O he is even in my mistress' case,
Just in her case. O woeful sympathy!
Piteous predicament! Even so lies she,
Blubb'ring and weeping, weeping and blubb'ring.
Stand up, stand up, stand, and you be a man;
For Juliet's sake, for her sake, rise and stand;
Why should you fall into so deep an O?

ROMEO
Nurse!

NURSE
Ah sir, ah sir! death's the end of all.

ROMEO
Spakest thou of Juliet? how is it with her?
Doth she not think me an old murderer,
Now I have stained the childhood of our joy
With blood removed but little from her own?
Where is she? and how doth she? and what says
My concealed lady to our cancelled love?

Knocking

Who is it? Where've you come from? What do you want?

NURSE
[Within] Let me in, and you'll know what
I want.
I've come from Juliet.

FRIAR LAWRENCE
In that case, you can come in.

Enter Nurse

NURSE
Oh, Friar Lawrence, Oh, tell me, Friar,
Where is Juliet's husband? Where is Romeo?

FRIAR LAWRENCE
There on the ground - drowning in floods of tears.

NURSE
Just like Juliet.
Exactly like her! Oh, how terrible!
What a terrible state of affairs! She's lying on her bed,
Weeping and wailing, wailing and weeping.
Get up. Get up! Get up and be a man.
For Juliet's sake, for her sake, get up now.
Why are you making such a noise?

ROMEO
Nurse!

NURSE
Ah, sir, sir! Death will resolve everything.

ROMEO
You mentioned Juliet? How is she?
Does she think I'm a murderer
Now I've ruined our newfound happiness
By shedding the blood of her cousin?
Where is she? And how is she? And what does
Juliet say about our cancelled plans?

NURSE
O she says nothing, sir, but weeps and weeps,
And now falls on her bed, and then starts up,
And Tybalt calls, and then on Romeo cries,
And then down falls again.

ROMEO
As if that name,
Shot from the deadly level of a gun,
Did murder her, as that name's cursed hand
Murdered her kinsman. O tell me, Friar, tell me,
In what vile part of this anatomy
Doth my name lodge? Tell me, that I may sack
The hateful mansion.

Drawing his sword

FRIAR LAWRENCE
Hold thy desperate hand!
Art thou a man? thy form cries out thou art;
Thy tears are womanish, thy wild acts denote
The unreasonable fury of a beast.
Unseemly woman in a seeming man,
And ill-beseeming beast in seeming both,
Thou hast amazed me. By my holy order,
I thought thy disposition better tempered.
Hast thou slain Tybalt? wilt thou slay thyself,
And slay thy lady thatin thy life lives,
By doing damnéd hate upon thyself?
Why rail'st thou on thy birth? the heaven, and earth?
Since birth, and heaven, and earth, all three do meet
In thee at once, which thou at once wouldst lose.
Fie, fie, thou shamest thy shape, thy love, thy wit,
Which like a usurer abound'st in all,
And usest none in that true use indeed
Which should bedeck thy shape, thy love, thy wit:
Thy noble shape is but a form of wax,
Digressing from the valour of a man;
Thy dear love sworn but hollow perjury,
Killing that love which thou hast vowed to cherish;
Thy wit, that ornament to shape and love,
Misshapen in the conduct of them both,

NURSE
Oh, she says nothing, sir, but cries and cries
And falls down on her bed. And then looks up,
And calls Tybalt, and then calls your name,
And then falls down again.

ROMEO
As if that name
Was a bullet that had been shot from a gun
And killed her. Because that name is the man who
Killed her cousin. Tell me, Friar, tell me
In what vile part of my body
Would I find my name? Tell me, so that I can cut off
That horrible part.

Drawing his sword

FRIAR LAWRENCE
Woah! Wait a minute!
Are you a man? You look like you are
But you're crying like a woman. Your mad actions suggest
The uncontrollable wildness of an animal.
The undesirable traits of woman in a respectable man!
Or an unpleasant animal in a seemingly pleasant human!
You amaze me. I swear,
I thought you had more sense than that.
You already killed Tybalt. Yet you'll kill yourself?
And thus kill the woman who lives for you
By inflicting punishment on yourself?
Why so angry about being born, about God, about life?
Since your birth, and God, and life, all combined
To create you and yet you'd willingly give it up.
Shame on you disrespecting your health, love, cleverness
Which, like a wealthy man, you have plenty of
And yet don't use any of it like you should -
Which would show you respect these attributes.
A body is just a temporary thing,
It diminishes the greatness of a man.
You have sworn your love but would break it
And by doing so kill the love that you vowed to protect.
Your cleverness, which compliments your health and love,
Is destroyed by misuse -

Like powder in a skilless soldier's flask,
Is set afire by thine own ignorance,
And thou dismembered with thine own defence.
What, rouse thee, man! thy Juliet is alive,
For whose dear sake thou wast but lately dead:
There art thou happy. Tybalt would kill thee,
But thou slewest Tybalt: there are thou happy.
The law that threatened death becomes thy friend,
And turns it to exile: there art thou happy.
A pack of blessings lights up upon thy back,
Happiness courts thee in her best array,
But like a misbehaved and sullen wench,
Thou pouts upon thy fortune and thy love:
Take heed, take heed, for such die miserable.
Go get thee to thy love as was decreed,
Ascend her chamber, hence and comfort her;
But look thou stay not till the watch be set,
For then thou canst not pass to Mantua,
Where thou shalt live till we can find a time
To blaze your marriage, reconcile your friends,
Beg pardon of the Prince, and call thee back
With twenty hundred thousand times more joy
Than thou went'st forth in lamentation.
Go before, Nurse, commend me to thy lady,
And bid her hasten all the house to bed,
Which heavy sorrow makes them apt unto.
Romeo is coming.

NURSE
O Lord, I could have stayed here all the night
To hear good counsel. O, what learning is!
My lord, I'll tell my lady you will come.

ROMEO
Do so, and bid my sweet prepare to chide.

NURSE
Here, sir, a ring she bid me give you, sir.
Hie you, make haste, for it grows very late.

Exit

Like ability in a skill-less man's hands,
Misused through his own ignorance -
And you are undone by your own actions.
Don't be so stupid! Juliet is alive -
For whose love you wish you were dead.
That's a good thing. Tybalt would have killed you,
But you killed Tybalt. That's a good thing.
The law which should have meant death let you off
And instead became banishment. That's a good thing.
A lot of good things to be grateful for -
You have been very lucky.
But, like a rude and petulant child,
You reject your good luck and your love.
Listen, otherwise you'll die miserable,
Go and be with Juliet, as you planned.
Go to her room now and comfort her
But make sure you're gone before the guards come on duty
Because then you won't be able to get to Mantua -
Where you'll have to live until we can find a way
To make your marriage public, reconcile your friends,
Beg the Prince for forgiveness, and get you brought back
Twenty hundred thousand times as happy
As when you left under such a dark cloud.
Go on ahead, Nurse. Send my greetings to Juliet
And tell her to get everyone in the house to go to bed,
Which their sorrow will make them eager to do.
Romeo is coming.

NURSE
Oh, Lord, I would have stayed here all night
To hear such good news. What a wonderful thing to hear!
Romeo, I'll tell Juliet you're coming.

ROMEO
Please do. And tell her to be prepared.

NURSE
Here, sir - this is a ring she asked me to give you, sir.
Please be quick - it's getting very late.

Exit

ROMEO
How well my comfort is revived by this.

FRIAR LAWRENCE
Go hence, good night, and here stands all your state:
Either be gone before the Watch be set,
Or by the break of day disguised from hence:
Sojourn in Mantua; I'll find out your man,
And he shall signify from time to time
Every good hap to you that chances here.
Give me thy hand, 'tis late. Farewell, good night.

ROMEO
But that a joy past joy calls out on me,
It were a grief, so brief to part with thee:
Farewell.

Exeunt

ROMEO
How much better I feel about it all!

FRIAR LAWRENCE
Go now. Good night. Remember this is what you must do -
Either be gone before the guards come on duty
Or at sunrise leave in disguise.
Wait in Mantua. I'll find your servant
And he'll notify you from time to time
Of everything that happens here that is good news for you.
Give me your hand. It's late. Goodbye. Good night.

ROMEO
If it weren't for something so wonderful waiting for me,
I'd be reluctant to leave you. Goodbye.

Exeunt

ACT III SCENE IV. A room in Capulet's house.

Enter CAPULET, LADY CAPULET, and PARIS

CAPULET
Things have fall'n out, sir, so unluckily
That we have had no time to move our daughter.
Look you, she loved her kinsman Tybalt dearly,
And so did I. Well, we were born to die.
'Tis very late, she'll not come down tonight.
I promise you, but for your company,
I would have been abed an hour ago.

PARIS
These times of woe afford no time to woo.
Madam, good night, commend me to your daughter.

LADY CAPULET
I will, and know her mind early tomorrow;
Tonight she is mewed up to her heaviness.

CAPULET
Sir Paris, I will make a desperate tender
Of my child's love: I think she will be ruled
In all respects by me; nay more, I doubt it not.
Wife, go you to her ere you go to bed,
Acquaint her here of my son Paris' love,
And bid her - mark you me? - on Wednesday next--
But, soft, what day is this?

PARIS
Monday, my lord.

CAPULET
Monday, ha, ha! Well, Wednesday is too soon,
A'Thursday let it be - a'Thursday, tell her,
She shall be married to this noble earl.
Will you be ready? do you like this haste?
We'll keep no great ado - a friend or two,
For hark you, Tybalt being slain so late,
It may be thought we held him carelessly,
Being our kinsman, if we revel much:
Therefore we'll have some half a dozen friends,
And there an end. But what say you to Thursday?

ACT III SCENE IV. A room in Capulet's house.

Enter CAPULET, LADY CAPULET, and PARIS

CAPULET
The things that have happened, Paris, are so unfortunate
That I haven't had a chance to speak to my daughter.
You know she loved her cousin Tybalt dearly -
As did I. Yet we all have to die.
It's very late. She won't come down tonight.
If it weren't for the fact that you're here,
I'd have been in bed an hour ago.

PARIS
These sad times don't allow for wooing.
Good night, madam. Send my greetings to your daughter.

LADY CAPULET
I will. And I'll speak to her early tomorrow.
Tonight she's all caught up in her sadness.

CAPULET
Paris, I'll be so bold as to say how I think
Juliet's feels. I think she will do
What I tell her and more - I don't doubt it.
Wife, go to her before you go to bed
And tell her about Paris's affection.
And tell her - are you listening? - next Wednesday -
Wait! What day is it?

PARIS
Monday, sir.

CAPULET
Monday! Hmm! Then Wednesday is too soon.
On Thursday then. On Thursday, tell her,
She will be married to this man.
Is that all right? Is it too soon?
We won't have a big wedding - one or two friends.
Because, I know, with Tybalt only recently dead,
It might be thought we don't care for him much,
Even though he's our relative, if we have a big celebration.
Therefore we'll have about half a dozen friends
And that'll be it. How does Thursday sound to you?

PARIS
My lord, I would that Thursday were tomorrow.

CAPULET
Well get you gone, a"Thursday be it, then. -
Go you to Juliet ere you go to bed,
Prepare her, wife, against this wedding day.
Farewell, my lord. Light to my chamber, ho!
Afore me, it is so very very late
That we may call it early by and by.
Good night.

Exeunt

PARIS
Sir, I wish it was Thursday tomorrow.

CAPULET
Good, that's settled then. On Thursday it'll be.
Go to Juliet before you go to bed,
Tell her to be ready, wife, for her wedding day.
Goodbye, Paris. Someone take a light to my room, now!
Goodness me! It's so late
That you could almost say it's early.
Goodnight.

Exeunt

ACT III SCENE V. Capulet's orchard.

Enter ROMEO and JULIET above, at the window

JULIET
Wilt thou be gone? it is not yet near day:
It was the nightingale, and not the lark,
That pierced the fearful hollow of thine ear;
Nightly she sings on yon pomegranate tree.
Believe me, love, it was the nightingale.

ROMEO
It was the lark, the herald of the morn,
No nightingale. Look, love, what envious streaks
Do lace the severing clouds in yonder east:
Night's candles are burnt out, and jocund day
Stands tiptoe on the misty mountain tops.
I must be gone and live, or stay and die.

JULIET
Yond light is not daylight, I know it, I:
It is some meteor that the sun exhaled,
To be to thee this night a torch-bearer,
And light thee on thy way to Mantua.
Therefore stay yet, thou need'st not to be gone.

ROMEO
Let me be tane, let me be put to death,
I am content, so thou wilt have it so.
I'll say yon grey is not the morning's eye,
'Tis but the pale reflex of Cynthia's brow;
Nor that is not the lark whose notes do beat
The vaulty heaven so high above our heads.
I have more care to stay than will to go:
Come, death, and welcome! Juliet wills it so.
How is't, my soul? Let's tal,; it is not day.

JULIET
It is, it is, hie hence, be gone, away!
It is the lark that sings so out of tune,
Straining harsh discords and unpleasing sharps.
Some say the lark makes sweet division;
This doth not so, for she divideth us.

ACT III SCENE V. Capulet's orchard.

Enter ROMEO and JULIET above, at the window

JULIET
Do you have to go? It's not daytime yet.
It was a nightingale, and not a lark,
That you heard just now.
It sings every night from the pomegranate tree.
Believe me, darling, it was a nightingale.

ROMEO
It was a lark - that indicates morning -
Not a nightingale. Look, darling, at the streaks of sunlight
That are striping across the clouds in the east.
Night time is over and the daylight
Is peeking over the hilltops.
I must go if I want to live. If I stay, I'll be killed.

JULIET
That light isn't daylight, I know so.
It is a meteor created by the sun
To provide you with light
To help you find your way to Mantua.
So stay - you don't need to go yet.

ROMEO
Let me be caught, let me be killed -
I am willing for that to happen.
That light is not the sunrise -
It's just a reflection of the moon.
And that isn't a lark that can be heard
Echoing in the sky above us.
I would much rather stay than go.
I'll gladly welcome death. If that's what you want.
What do you think, darling? Let's talk. It's not daytime yet.

JULIET
But it is, it is. Quick! Get going, go!
It was a lark that sang so harshly -
Belting out her tuneless notes and horrible sound.
Some say a lark sounds sweet
But that isn't true because it means we have to part.

Some say the lark and loathéd toad changed eyes,
O now I would they had changed voices too,
Since arm from arm that voice doth us affray,
Hunting thee hence with hunt's-up to the day.
O now be gone; more light and light it grows.

ROMEO
More light and light, more dark and dark our woes!

Enter Nurse, to the chamber

NURSE
Madam!

JULIET
Nurse?

NURSE
Your lady mother is coming to your chamber.
The day is broke, be wary, look about.

Exit

JULIET
Then, window, let day in, and let life out.

ROMEO
Farewell, farewell! one kiss, and I'll descend.

He goeth down

JULIET
Art thou gone so, love, lord, ay husband, friend?
I must hear from thee every day in the hour,
For in a minute there are many days.
O, by this count I shall be much in years
Ere I again behold my Romeo!

ROMEO
Farewell!
I will omit no opportunity
That may convey my greetings, love, to thee.

JULIET
O think'st thou we shall ever meet again?

It's said the lark changed eyes with a toad -
I wish now that they had changed voices too
As that sound forces us apart -
Forcing you from here by signifying the start of the day.
Go on, go - it's getting lighter and lighter.

ROMEO
The lighter it gets, the heavier our spirits.

Enter Nurse, to the chamber

NURSE
Juliet!

JULIET
Nurse?

NURSE
Your mother is coming to your room.
It's morning. Be alert, take care.

Exit

JULIET
Then the window that let the daylight in will let you out.

ROMEO
Goodbye, goodbye. One last kiss and I'll go.

He goeth down

JULIET
You're gone so quick. My love, master, husband, friend!
I must hear from you every hour of every day
For a minute can seem like days
And for me it will seem like years
Before I can see Romeo again!

ROMEO
Goodbye!
I will not miss any opportunity
That I can find to send a message to you, darling.

JULIET
Do you think we will ever see each other again?

ROMEO
I doubt it not, and all these woes shall serve
For sweet discourses in our times to come.

JULIET
O God, I have an ill-divining soul!
Methinks I see thee now, thou art so low,
As one dead in the bottom of a tomb.
Either my eyesight fails, or thou look'st pale.

ROMEO
And trust me, love, in my eye so do you:
Dry sorrow drinks our blood. Adieu, adieu!

Exit

JULIET
O Fortune, Fortune, all men call thee fickle;
If thou art fickle, what dost thou with him
That is renowned for faith? Be fickle, Fortune:
For then I hope thou wilt not keep him long,
But send him back.

LADY CAPULET
[Within] Ho, daughter, are you up?

JULIET
Who is't that calls? It is my lady mother.
Is she not down so late, or up so early?
What unaccustomed cause procures her hither?

Enter LADY CAPULET

LADY CAPULET
Why how now, Juliet!

JULIET
Madam, I am not well.

LADY CAPULET
Evermore weeping for your cousin's death?
What, wilt thou wash him from his grave with tears?
And if thou couldst, thou couldst not make him live;

ROMEO
I don't doubt it. And all this sadness will prove
To be trivial to us in the future.

JULIET
Oh God, I have a bad feeling.
From where I am it looks like you are lying
In a tomb like a corpse.
And, either my eyesight's failing, or you look pale.

ROMEO
And believe me, darling, you look the same to me.
Our sorrow is sapping our spirit. Goodbye, Goodbye!

Exit

JULIET
People say that luck is changeable.
If it is changeable, how can it be so cruel to someone
So honourable? I hope my luck will be changeable
Because then it won't be long
Before Romeo can come back.

LADY CAPULET
[Within] Hello, Juliet! Are you awake?

JULIET
Who is that? Is that my mother?
She's either stayed up very late, or she's up very early?
What on earth brings her here?

Enter LADY CAPULET

LADY CAPULET
Ah, how are you, Juliet?

JULIET
I'm not well, Mum.

LADY CAPULET
Still crying over your cousin's death?
You'll wash him out of his grave with all your tears?
And, even if you could, you couldn't make him live again.

Therefore have done. Some grief shows much of love,
But much of grief shows still some want of wit.

JULIET
Yet let me weep for such a feeling loss.

LADY CAPULET
So shall you feel the loss, but not the friend
Which you weep for.

JULIET
Feeling so the loss,
I cannot choose but ever weep the friend.

LADY CAPULET
Well, girl, thou weep'st not so much for his death,
As that the villain lives which slaughtered him.

JULIET
What villain, madam?

LADY CAPULET
That same villain Romeo.

JULIET
[Aside] Villain and he be many miles asunder. -
God pardon him, I do, with all my heart:
And yet no man like he doth grieve my heart.

LADY CAPULET
That is because the traitor murderer lives.

JULIET
Ay, madam, from the reach of these my hands.
Would none but I might venge my cousin's death!

LADY CAPULET
We will have vengeance for it, fear thou not:
Then weep no more. I'll send to one in Mantua,
Where that same banished runagate doth live,
Shall give him such an unaccustomed dram,
That he shall soon keep Tybalt company;
And then I hope thou wilt be satisfied.

So no more. Some sadness suggests you loved him dearly.
But too much suggests you don't have much brain.

JULIET
Just let me weep for my feeling of loss.

LADY CAPULET
You might feel the loss but you'll never feel the person
You're crying for.

JULIET
If I feel the loss,
I can't help but cry for the person.

LADY CAPULET
Well, dear, you won't cry as much as you are over him,
When you hear that the man who killed him still lives.

JULIET
What man, mum?

LADY CAPULET
That evil man, Romeo.

JULIET
[Aside] He's evil to be so far away.
God forgive him! I do, with all my heart.
And yet no-one makes my heart ache like him.

LADY CAPULET
That is because his murderer still lives.

JULIET
Yes, mum, but too far for me to reach.
I wish I could avenge my cousin's death!

LADY CAPULET
We will have vengeance for it, don't worry.
So no more crying. I'll send someone to Mantua,
Where that banished criminal lives,
Who will slip him such a powerful poison
That he will soon join Tybalt in the afterlife.
And then, I hope, that will make you happy.

JULIET
Indeed I never shall be satisfied
With Romeo, till I behold him – dead -
Is my poor heart, so for a kinsman vexed.
Madam, if you could find out but a man
To bear a poison, I would temper it,
That Romeo should upon receipt thereof
Soon sleep in quiet. O, how my heart abhors
To hear him named, and cannot come to him,
To wreak the love I bore my cousin
Upon his body that slaughtered him!

LADY CAPULET
Find thou the means, and I'll find such a man.
But now I'll tell thee joyful tidings, girl.

JULIET
And joy comes well in such a needy time.
What are they, beseech your ladyship?

LADY CAPULET
Well, well, thou hast a careful father, child,
One who, to put thee from thy heaviness,
Hath sorted out a sudden day of joy,
That thou expects not, nor I looked not for.

JULIET
Madam, in happy time, what day is that?

LADY CAPULET
Marry, my child, early next Thursday morn,
The gallant, young, and noble gentleman,
The County Paris, at Saint Peter's Church,
Shall happily make thee there a joyful bride.

JULIET
Now by Saint Peter's Church and Peter too,
He shall not make me there a joyful bride.
I wonder at this haste, that I must wed
Ere he that should be husband comes to woo.
I pray you tell my lord and father, madam,
I will not marry yet, and when I do, I swear,
It shall be Romeo, whom you know I hate,
Rather than Paris. These are news indeed!

JULIET
Quite. I shall never be happy
With Romeo until I see him – dead -
Is my poor heart for the loss of my cousin.
Mum, if you could find someone
To take the poison, I would alter it
So that Romeo would, on drinking it,
Soon be in a deep sleep. Oh, how I hate
To hear his name and not be able to see him.
To express the love I felt for my cousin
On the man that killed him!

LADY CAPULET
If you find the poison, I'll find someone to take it.
But now I've good news to tell you, my dear.

JULIET
Which is very welcome at such a terrible time.
What is it? Please tell me, mum.

LADY CAPULET
Well, you have a wonderful father, dear.
One who, to help you get over your sorrow,
Has arranged a day of happiness
That you didn't expect and I couldn't have hoped for.

JULIET
Come on, Mum, what do you mean?

LADY CAPULET
Why, darling, next Thursday morning,
The handsome, young and rich gentleman,
Count Paris, at Saint Peter's Church,
Will make you his lawful wife.

JULIET
What? At Saint Peter's Church and in front of St. Peter
He will not make me his lawful wife.
I'm amazed at this suddenness - that I must be married
Before the man who is to be my husband has wooed me.
Please tell my father, mum,
I won't get married yet. And, when I do, I promise,
I'd rather marry Romeo - who you know I hate -
Than Paris. What an astonishing thing to say!

LADY CAPULET
Here comes your father, tell him so yourself;
And see how he will take it at your hands.

Enter CAPULET and Nurse

CAPULET
When the sun sets, the air doth drizzle dew,
But for the sunset of my brother's son
It rains downright.
How now, a conduit, girl? What, still in tears?
Evermore show'ring? In one little body
Thou counterfeits a bark, a sea, a wind:
For still thy eyes, which I may call the sea,
Do ebb and flow with tears; the bark thy body is,
Sailing in this salt flood; the winds, thy sighs,
Who, raging with thy tears and they with them,
Without a sudden calm, will overset
Thy tempest-tossed body. How now, wife,
Have you delivered to her our decree?

LADY CAPULET
Ay, sir, but she will none, she gives you thanks.
I would the fool were married to her grave.

CAPULET
Soft, take me with you, take me with you, wife.
How, will she none? doth she not give us thanks?
Is she not proud? doth she not count her blest,
Unworthy as she is, that we have wrought
So worthy a gentleman to be her bride?

JULIET
Not proud you have, but thankful that you have:
Proud can I never be of what I hate,
But thankful even for hate that is meant love.

CAPULET
How now, how now, chop-logic? What is this?
'Proud', and 'I thank you', and 'I thank you not',
And yet 'not proud', mistress minion you,
Thank me no thankings, nor, proud me no prouds,
But fettle your fine joints 'gainst Thursday next,
To go with Paris to Saint Peter's Church,

LADY CAPULET
Here comes your father - you can tell him yourself
And see how he takes it coming from you.

Enter CAPULET and Nurse

CAPULET
When the sun sets the grass becomes damp with dew
But following the death of my nephew
It pours down.
Now then. What's this, girl? Still in tears?
Still crying? In your little body
You have enough to float a ship, fill a sea, cause a storm.
For your eyes still, like the sea,
Fill and run with water. Your body is the ship -
Set adrift by your tears. Your sighs are like the storm,
Which, combined with your tears, and they with your sighs
If they don't abate, will overcome
Your grief-stricken body. Now then, my dear,
Did you tell her our decision?

LADY CAPULET
Yes, dear. She said she's not interested, thank you.
I wish she was dead!

CAPULET
What? I agree with you, I agree with you, dear.
You say she won't do it? Isn't she grateful?
Isn't she pleased? Doesn't she consider herself blessed
That, for someone as undeserving as her, we got
Someone so wonderful to be her husband?

JULIET
I'm not pleased. But I am grateful.
I could never be pleased about something I hate.
But I am grateful because I know it was done with love.

CAPULET
What's this? Twisting my words! What's she saying?
'Pleased,' and 'thank you,' but 'no thank you'
And 'not pleased', you spoilt brat.
Don't thank me and don't be pleased
Just get yourself ready for next Thursday
To go with Paris to Saint Peter's Church

Or I will drag thee on a hurdle thither.
Out, you green-sickness carrion! out, you baggage!
You tallow-face!

LADY CAPULET
Fie, fie, what, are you mad?

JULIET
Good father, I beseech you on my knees,
Hear me with patience but to speak a word.

CAPULET
Hang thee, young baggage, disobedient wretch!
I tell thee what: get thee to church a'Thursday,
Or never after look me in the face.
Speak not, reply not, do not answer me!
My fingers itch. Wife, we scarce thought us blest
That God had lent us but this only child,
But now I see this one is one too much,
And that we have a curse in having her.
Out on her, hilding!

NURSE
God in heaven bless her!
You are to blame, my lord, to rate her so.

CAPULET
And why, my Lady Wisdom? Hold your tongue,
Good Prudence, smatter with your gossips, go.

NURSE
I speak no treason.

CAPULET
O God-i-goden!

NURSE
May not one speak?

CAPULET
Peace, you mumbling fool!
Utter your gravity o'er a gossip's bowl,
For here we need it not.

Or I will drag you there on a cart.
Get out, you sickly pile of flesh! Get out, waste of space!
You pale-faced girl!

LADY CAPULET
What! Have you gone mad?

JULIET
Please, father, I beg you on my knees,
Listen to what I have to say.

CAPULET
To hell with you, you waste of space! Disobedient cow!
I'll tell you this – get to church on Thursday
Or I will never look at you again.
Don't speak, don't reply, don't answer back
Or I will beat you. Dear, we thought we'd been blessed
When God gave us this one child
But now I see that even one is one too much
And that we have been cursed in having her.
Get out, you useless lump!

NURSE
God forgive her!
You are in the wrong, sir, for treating her like that.

CAPULET
What's this? Another smart Alec? Be quiet.
Be sensible. Save your drivel for your friends, go away.

NURSE
I'm telling the truth.

CAPULET
Oh, get lost.

NURSE
Can't I say something?

CAPULET
Shut up, you jabbering idiot!
Say what you have to say to your friends -
I don't want to hear it.

LADY CAPULET
You are too hot.

CAPULET
God's bread, it makes me mad!
Day, night, work, play,
Alone, in company, still my care hath been
To have her matched; and having now provided
A gentleman of noble parentage,
Of fair demesnes, youthful and nobly ligned,
Stuffed, as they say, with honourable parts,
Proportioned as one's thought would wish a man,
And then to have a wretched puling fool,
A whining mammet, in her fortune's tender,
To answer 'I'll not wed, I cannot love;
I am too young, I pray you, pardon me.'
But, as you will not wed, I'll pardon you:
Graze where you will, you shall not house with me.
Look to't, think on't, I do not use to jest.
Thursday is near, lay hand on heart, advise:
An you be mine, I'll give you to my friend;
And you be not, hang, beg, starve, die in
the streets,
For by my soul, I'll ne'er acknowledge thee,
Nor what is mine shall never do thee good.
Trust to't, bethink you, I'll not be forsworn.

Exit

JULIET
Is there no pity sitting in the clouds
That sees into the bottom of my grief?
O sweet my mother, cast me not away!
Delay this marriage for a month, a week,
Or if you do not, make the bridal bed
In that dim monument where Tybalt lies.

LADY CAPULET
Talk not to me, for I'll not speak a word.
Do as thou wilt, for I have done with thee.

Exit

LADY CAPULET
You're getting too worked up.

CAPULET
Good God! I don't believe it!
Day and night, all my life,
Whether on my own or with others I have sought only
To find her a husband. And now I've managed
To find a man from a noble family
Who's wealthy, young, and respectable,
Full, as they say, of many honourable qualities
With an appearance thought desirable in a man.
To have this pathetic sobbing fool,
This whining child, when faced with her good fortune,
To say 'I won't get married, I'm not in love,
I'm too young, please, forgive me.'
Fine, if you won't get married, I'll forgive you.
But you'll fend for yourself because you won't live here.
So there. Think about that. I'm not one to make jokes.
Thursday is not far away. I swear - listen to me -
If you are my daughter, you will marry Paris.
If you're not, then you can suffer, beg, starve, die in
the streets,
Because, I swear, I'll never admit you're my daughter
And nothing of mine will ever be used to help you.
You know it's true, because you know I won't be denied.

Exit

JULIET
Is there no-one at all
That understands how awful I'm feeling?
Oh, please, mother, don't abandon me!
Delay this marriage for a month, a week.
Or, if you don't, my wedding bed
Will the equivalent of my coffin.

LADY CAPULET
Don't talk to me - I won't say anything.
Do what you want. I won't have any more to do with you

Exit

JULIET
O God! - O Nurse, how shall this be prevented?
My husband is on earth, my faith in heaven;
How shall that faith return again to earth,
Unless that husband send it me from heaven
By leaving earth? Comfort me, counsel me.
Alack, alack, that heaven should practise stratagems
Upon so soft a subject as myself!
What say'st thou? hast thou not a word of joy?
Some comfort, Nurse.

NURSE
Faith, here it is:
Romeo is banished, and all the world to nothing
That he dares ne'er come back to challenge you;
Or if he do, it needs must be by stealth.
Then, since the case so stands as now it doth,
I think it best you married with the County.
O, he's a lovely gentleman!
Romeo's a dishclout to him. An eagle, madam,
Hath not so green, so quick, so fair an eye
As Paris hath. Beshrew my very heart,
I think you are happy in this second match,
For it excels your first, or if it did not,
Your first is dead, or 'twere as good he were
As living here and you no use of him.

JULIET
Speak'st thou from thy heart?

NURSE
And from my soul too,
else beshrew them both.

JULIET
Amen!

NURSE
What?

JULIET
Well, thou hast comforted me marvellous much.
Go in, and tell my lady I am gone,
Having displeased my father, to Lawrence' cell,
To make confession and to be absolved.

JULIET
Oh, God! Nurse, what can we do to stop this?
My husband is still alive. I have faith in God.
But how can God help me
Unless he does so by taking Romeo
To heaven? Say something to comfort me, advise me.
Oh dear, oh dear. That God could be so cruel
To someone as fragile as me!
What have you to say? Haven't you any words of comfort?
Something to help me, Nurse.

NURSE
All right, here it is.
Romeo is banished and it'll mean the end for him
If he dares to come back to find you.
And, if he does, it must be done by stealth.
So, since things stand as they are,
I think it would be best if you married Count Paris.
He's a lovely man!
Romeo's nothing compared to him. Even a king, Juliet,
Does not have such beautiful, sharp, and fine eyes
As Paris. I swear,
I think you'll be happier in this second marriage,
It's much better than your first. And, if it isn't,
Your first husband is dead. Or as good as dead
If he comes back - you can't be with him.

JULIET
Is this what you really think?

NURSE
I swear.
Otherwise condemn me to hell.

JULIET
I'll agree to that!

NURSE
What?

JULIET
Well, you've been a great comfort to me.
Go inside and tell my mother I've gone,
Having upset my father, to Friar Lawrence's church
To confess this sin and be absolved.

NURSE
Marry, I will, and this is wisely done.

Exit

JULIET
Ancient damnation! O most wicked fiend!
Is it more sin to wish me thus forsworn,
Or to dispraise my lord with that same tongue
Which she hath praised him with above compare
So many thousand times? Go, counsellor,
Thou and my bosom henceforth shall be twain.
I'll to the Friar, to know his remedy;
If all else fail, myself have power to die.

Exit

NURSE
Yes, I will. I think it's a good idea.

Exit

JULIET
How dare she! It's so terrible of her!
How can she suggest I ignore my vows
Or disparage my husband with the same tongue
Which praised him above compare
So many times? You can get lost, Nurse.
You and I shall never again be close friends.
I'll go to Friar Lawrence to ask his advice.
If all else fails, I am willing to die.

Exit

ACT IV SCENE I. Friar Lawrence's cell.

Enter FRIAR LAWRENCE and PARIS

FRIAR LAWRENCE
On Thursday, sir? the time is very short.

PARIS
My father Capulet will have it so,
And I am nothing slow to slack his haste.

FRIAR LAWRENCE
You say you do not know the lady's mind?
Uneven is the course, I like it not.

PARIS
Immoderately she weeps for Tybalt's death,
And therefore have I little talked of love,
For Venus smiles not in a house of tears.
Now, sir, her father counts it dangerous
That she doth give her sorrow so much sway;
And in his wisdom hastes our marriage
To stop the inundation of her tears,
Which too much minded by herself alone
May be put from her by society.
Now do you know the reason of this haste.

FRIAR LAWRENCE
[Aside] I would I knew not why it should be slowed. -
Look, sir, here comes the lady towards my cell.

Enter JULIET

PARIS
Happily met, my lady and my wife!

JULIET
That may be, sir, when I may be a wife.

PARIS
That 'may be' must be, love, on Thursday next.

JULIET
What must be shall be.

ACT IV SCENE I. Friar Lawrence's cell.

Enter FRIAR LAWRENCE and PARIS

FRIAR LAWRENCE
On Thursday, sir? That's not far away.

PARIS
Mr Capulet has decided it will be so.
And I wouldn't want to argue with him.

FRIAR LAWRENCE
You say you do not know how Juliet feels about it.
It seems very unfair. I don't like it.

PARIS
She cries a lot over Tybalt's death.
And so I haven't talked a lot to her about love
Because love isn't generally welcomed by grieving people.
But, sir, her father doesn't consider it right
That she is allowing her sorrow to overcome her
And he has decided to bring forward our marriage
To stop her crying so much -
Which has led to her spending too much time alone
And has distanced her from society.
So now you know the reason for the rush.

FRIAR LAWRENCE
[Aside] I wish I didn't know why it needs to be delayed.
Look, sir, here comes Juliet approaching my church.

Enter JULIET

PARIS
How lovely to see you, my beautiful wife!

JULIET
That may be true, sir, when I am your wife.

PARIS
That 'may be' will happen, darling – on Thursday.

JULIET
What must happen will happen.

FRIAR LAWRENCE
That's a certain text.

PARIS
Come you to make confession to this father?

JULIET
To answer that, I should confess to you.

PARIS
Do not deny to him that you love me.

JULIET
I will confess to you that I love him.

PARIS
So will ye, I am sure, that you love me.

JULIET
If I do so, it will be of more price,
Being spoke behind your back, than to your face.

PARIS
Poor soul, thy face is much abused with tears.

JULIET
The tears have got small victory by that,
For it was bad enough before their spite.

PARIS
Thou wrong'st it more than tears with that report.

JULIET
That is no slander, sir, which is a truth,
And what I spake, I spake it to my face.

PARIS
Thy face is mine, and thou hast slandered it.

JULIET
It may be so, for it is not mine own.
Are you at leisure, holy father, now;
Or shall I come to you at evening mass?

FRIAR LAWRENCE
That's very true.

PARIS
Have you come to make confession to Friar Lawrence?

JULIET
To answer that I'd need to tell you my confession.

PARIS
Don't deny to him that you love me.

JULIET
I will admit to you that I love him.

PARIS
And you will, I am sure, say that you love me.

JULIET
If I do, it will mean more -
Being said to someone other than you.

PARIS
Poor thing, your face is stained in tears.

JULIET
That's a good thing.
It looked bad enough before I cried.

PARIS
By saying that you're being even more unkind to it.

JULIET
It's not unfair, sir, if it's true.
And what I said, I said openly.

PARIS
You are mine. And thus you have insulted my property.

JULIET
That may true, for it is not truly me.
Are you free now, Friar Lawrence.
Or should I come back at the evening service?

FRIAR LAWRENCE
My leisure serves me, pensive daughter, now.
My lord, we must entreat the time alone.

PARIS
God shield I should disturb devotion!
Juliet, on Thursday early will I rouse ye;
Till then adieu, and keep this holy kiss.

Exit

JULIET
O shut the door, and when thou hast done so,
Come weep with me, past hope, past cure, past help!

FRIAR LAWRENCE
O Juliet, I already know thy grief,
It strains me past the compass of my wits.
I hear thou must, and nothing may prorogue it,
On Thursday next be married to this County.

JULIET
Tell me not, Friar, that thou hearest of this,
Unless thou tell me how I may prevent it.
If in thy wisdom thou canst give no help,
Do thou but call my resolution wise,
And with this knife I'll help it presently.
God joined my heart and Romeo's, thou our hands,
And ere this hand, by thee to Romeo sealed,
Shall be the label to another deed,
Or my true heart with treacherous revolt
Turn to another, this shall slay them both:
Therefore, out of thy long-experienced time,
Give me some present counsel, or, behold,
'Twixt my extremes and me this bloody knife
Shall play the umpire, arbitrating that
Which the commission of thy years and art
Could to no issue of true honour bring.
Be not so long to speak, I long to die,
If what thou speak'st speak not of remedy.

FRIAR LAWRENCE
I'm free now, my child.
Paris, we must be left alone.

PARIS
God forbid I should interrupt religious devotion!
Juliet, early next Thursday I'll come find you.
Until then, goodbye. And remember me with this kiss.

Exit

JULIET
Shut the door! And, when you have,
Come cry with me. I'm past hope, past solution, past help!

FRIAR LAWRENCE
Ah, Juliet, I already know your problem.
I find it almost beyond belief.
I've heard you must - and nothing can delay it -
Be married to Paris next Thursday.

JULIET
Don't tell me, Friar, that you've heard this
Unless you know how I can prevent it.
If, with all your knowledge, you can't think of anything
Then I hope you'll understand my decision
To use this knife to resolve it.
Romeo and I were joined in holy matrimony by you
And before I, who you married to Romeo,
Will agree to marry someone else,
Or my heart like a traitor
Falls for someone else, I will kill myself.
Therefore, from your considerable experience,
Give me some advice or watch
As, to determine my fate, this knife
Will make the decision - resolving the problem
To which, with all your years of knowledge and skill,
You couldn't find another solution.
Speak quickly. I am prepared to die
If what you have to say won't help.

FRIAR LAWRENCE
Hold, daughter, I do spy a kind of hope,
Which craves as desperate an execution.
As that is desperate which we would prevent.
If, rather than to marry County Paris,
Thou hast the strength of will to slay thyself,
Then is it likely thou wilt undertake
A thing like death to chide away this shame,
That cop'st with Death himself to scape from it;
And, if thou dar'st, I'll give thee remedy.

JULIET
O bid me leap, rather than marry Paris,
From off the battlements of any tower,
Or walk in thievish ways, or bid me lurk
Where serpents are; chain me with roaring bears,
Or shut me nightly in a charnel-house,
O'ercovered quite with dead men's rattling bones,
With reeky shanks and yellow chapless skulls;
Or bid me go into a new-made grave,
And hide me with a dead man in his shroud -
Things that to hear them told have made me tremble -
And I will do it without fear or doubt,
To live an unstained wife to my sweet love.

FRIAR LAWRENCE
Hold then, go home, be merry, give consent
To marry Paris. Wednesday is tomorrow;
Tomorrow night look that thou lie alone,
Let not the Nurse lie with thee in thy chamber.
Take thou this vial, being then in bed,
And this distilled liquor drink thou off,
When presently through all thy veins shall run
A cold and drowsy humour; for no pulse
Shall keep his native progress, but surcease;
No warmth, no breath, shall testify thou livest;
The roses in thy lips and cheeks shall fade
To wanny ashes, thy eyes' windows fall,
Like Death when he shuts up the day of life;
Each part, deprived of supple government,
Shall, stiff and stark and cold, appear like death,
And in this borrowed likeness of shrunk death
Thou shalt continue two and forty hours,
And then awake as from a pleasant sleep.
Now when the bridegroom in the morning comes

FRIAR LAWRENCE
Wait, child. I can think of something that might help,
Which requires measures as extreme
As your desperation to avoid your fate.
If, rather than marry Paris,
You are prepared to kill yourself,
Then is it likely you'd be prepared to agree to
Something like death to solve this problem -
That you are prepared to meet with death to escape from.
And, if you will, I'll give you a solution.

JULIET
I'd do anything rather than marry Paris -
Even jump off the top of any tower.
Or turn to crime. Or live
With snakes. Or be put in a cage with bears.
Or be locked every night in a crypt
And covered with the bones of dead men,
With their stinking remains and yellow jawless skulls.
Or ask me to get into a newly-dug grave
And lie down with a dead man in his coffin.
Things that, before, would have made me tremble
I would now do without fear or hesitation
To prevent myself having to betray Romeo.

FRIAR LAWRENCE
In that case, go home, be happy, and agree
To marry Paris. It's Wednesday tomorrow.
Tomorrow night make sure you're left alone -
Don't let the nurse stay with you in your room.
Take this little bottle and, when you're in bed,
Drink all of the liquid that's inside it.
You'll soon start to feel
Cold and drowsy. Your pulse
Won't keep its usual beat - it'll stop.
No warmth and no breath will indicate you're alive.
The colour in your lips and cheeks will fade
To pale grey. The light will fade from your eyes
Like when death causes a body to shut down.
Each part of your body will be immovable -
Stiff and stark and cold like a corpse -
And in this apparent deathlike state
You'll remain for forty two hours
And then wake up as if from a pleasant sleep.
But, when Paris comes in the morning

To rouse thee from thy bed, there art thou dead.
Then as the manner of our country is,
In thy best robes, uncovered on the bier
Thou shalt be borne to that same ancient vault
Where all the kindred of the Capulets lie.
In the mean time, against thou shalt awake,
Shall Romeo by my letters know our drift,
And hither shall he come, and he and I
Will watch thy waking, and that very night
Shall Romeo bear thee hence to Mantua.
And this shall free thee from this present shame,
If no inconstant toy, nor womanish fear,
Abate thy valour in the acting it.

JULIET
Give me, give me! O tell not me of fear.

FRIAR LAWRENCE
Hold, get you gone, be strong and prosperous
In this resolve; I'll send a friar with speed
To Mantua, with my letters to thy lord.

JULIET
Love give me strength, and strength shall help afford.
Farewell, dear father.

Exeunt

To wake you up, he'll find you dead.
Then, as is the custom in our country,
In your best clothes and on a funeral litter
You'll be taken to the same tomb
Where all the relatives of the Capulets are buried.
In the meantime, before you wake up,
Romeo will hear of our plan from my letters.
And he'll come here and he and I
Will wait for you to wake up. And that night
Romeo will take you back to Mantua
And you'll be free from your present problem.
So long as you don't let doubt or womanly cowardice
Diminish your determination to do it.

JULIET
Give it to me, give it to me! I am not afraid!

FRIAR LAWRENCE
Alright. Now get going. Be brave and be determined
To do this. I'll send a Friar immediately
To Mantua with letters for Romeo.

JULIET
My love gives me strength! Strength will help me do this.
Goodbye, Friar!

Exeunt

ACT IV SCENE II. Hall in Capulet's house.

Enter CAPULET, LADY CAPULET, Nurse, and two Servingmen

CAPULET
So many guests invite as here are writ.

Exit First Servant

Sirrah, go hire me twenty cunning cooks.

Second Servant
You shall have none ill, sir, for I'll try if they can lick their fingers.

CAPULET
How canst thou try them so?

Second Servant
Marry, sir, 'tis an ill cook that cannot lick his own fingers; therefore he that cannot lick his fingers goes not with me.

CAPULET
Go, be gone.

Exit Second Servant

We shall be much unfurnished for this time.
What, is my daughter gone to Friar Lawrence?

NURSE
Ay forsooth.

CAPULET
Well, he may chance to do some good on her.
A peevish self-willed harlotry it is.

NURSE
See where she comes from shrift with merry look.

Enter JULIET

CAPULET
How now, my headstrong, where have you been gadding?

ACT IV SCENE II. Hall in Capulet's house.

Enter CAPULET, LADY CAPULET, Nurse, and two Servingmen

CAPULET
Invite everyone on this list.

Exit First Servant

You - go and hire twenty good cooks.

Second Servant
You'll have the very best, sir, because I'll ask if they
Are prepared to lick their fingers.

CAPULET
Why would you do that?

Second Servant
Because, sir, a bad cook won't eat their
own cooking. Therefore any that won't lick their
fingers won't be good enough.

CAPULET
Go on, go.

Exit Second Servant

We won't be ready in time.
Has Juliet gone to Friar Lawrence?

NURSE
Yes, she has.

CAPULET
Good, he might make her see sense.
Troublesome, stubborn little madam that she is.

NURSE
Look, she's back now and seems much happier.

Enter JULIET

CAPULET
Hello, my headstrong daughter! Where have you been?

JULIET
Where I have learnt me to repent the sin
Of disobedient opposition
To you and your behests, and am enjoined
By holy Lawrence to fall prostrate here
To beg your pardon. Pardon, I beseech you!
Henceforward I am ever ruled by you.

CAPULET
Send for the County, go tell him of this.
I'll have this knot knit up to-morrow morning.

JULIET
I met the youthful lord at Lawrence' cell,
And gave him what becomed love I might,
Not stepping o'er the bounds of modesty.

CAPULET
Why, I am glad on't, this is well, stand up.
This is as't should be. Let me see the County;
Ay, marry, go, I say, and fetch him hither.
Now afore God, this reverend holy Friar,
All our whole city is much bound to him.

JULIET
Nurse, will you go with me into my closet,
To help me sort such needful ornaments
As you think fit to furnish me tomorrow?

LADY CAPULET
No, not till Thursday, there is time enough.

CAPULET
Go, Nurse, go with her, we'll to church tomorrow.

Exeunt JULIET and Nurse

LADY CAPULET
We shall be short in our provision,
'Tis now near night.

JULIET
Somewhere I learnt to regret
Being so disobedient
To you and your decisions. I've been told
By Friar Lawrence to fall to my knees
And beg your forgiveness. Forgive me, I beg you!
From now on I will always do what you say.

CAPULET
Go and get Paris and tell him about this.
We'll have this all sorted out tomorrow morning.

JULIET
I met Paris at Friar Lawrence's church
And gave him what signs of affection were right
Without overstepping what would be acceptable.

CAPULET
I'm glad about that. That's good. Stand up.
Everything's how it should be. I must speak to Paris.
Yes, go, I said, and bring him here.
I swear, this Friar Lawrence -
We owe a lot to him.

JULIET
Nurse, will you come with me to my wardrobe
To help me find the sort of thing
You think I should wear tomorrow?

LADY CAPULET
No, leave that until Thursday – there's plenty of time.

CAPULET
Go on, Nurse, go with her. We're off to church tomorrow.

Exeunt JULIET and Nurse

LADY CAPULET
We won't be ready.
It's nearly night time.

CAPULET
Tush, I will stir about,
And all things shall be well, I warrant thee, wife:
Go thou to Juliet, help to deck up her;
I'll not to bed tonight; let me alone,
I'll play the huswife for this once. What ho!
They are all forth. Well, I will walk myself
To County Paris, to prepare up him
Against tomorrow. My heart is wondrous light,
Since this same wayward girl is so reclaimed.

Exeunt

CAPULET
Rubbish, I'll keep working
And everything will be alright. I promise you, dear.
Go to Juliet - help her get ready.
I'll stay up tonight. Let me get on.
I'll do your job just this once. What's this?
All the servants are busy? In that case, I'll go myself
To Paris to get him ready
For tomorrow. I feel much happier
Since that disobedient girl started behaving herself.

Exeunt

ACT IV SCENE III. Juliet's chamber.

Enter JULIET and Nurse

JULIET
Ay, those attires are best, but, gentle Nurse,
I pray thee leave me to my self to-night:
For I have need of many orisons
To move the heavens to smile upon my state,
Which, well thou knowest, is cross and full of sin.

Enter LADY CAPULET

LADY CAPULET
What, are you busy, ho? need you my help?

JULIET
No, madam, we have culled such necessaries
As are behoveful for our state to-morrow.
So please you, let me now be left alone,
And let the Nurse this night sit up with you,
For I am sure you have your hands full all,
In this so sudden business.

LADY CAPULET
Good night.
Get thee to bed, and rest, for thou hast need.

Exeunt LADY CAPULET and Nurse

JULIET
Farewell! God knows when we shall meet again.
I have a faint cold fear thrills through my veins
That almost freezes up the heat of life:
I'll call them back again to comfort me.
Nurse! - What should she do here?
My dismal scene I needs must act alone.
Come, vial.
What if this mixture do not work at all?
Shall I be married then tomorrow morning?
No, no, this shall forbid it; lie thou there.

Laying down her dagger

ACT IV SCENE III. Juliet's chamber.

Enter JULIET and Nurse

JULIET
Yes, those clothes are best. But, Nurse,
Please leave me on my own tonight.
I have many prayers I need to say
To get God to give me his blessing
Because, as you know, I've done a lot to make him angry.

Enter LADY CAPULET

LADY CAPULET
Hello, are you alright in there? Do you need my help?

JULIET
No, mum, we've picked out the items
That are suitable for my wedding tomorrow.
So, please, leave me alone now
And let the nurse stay with you tonight.
Because I am sure you have a lot to do
What with all that's happened.

LADY CAPULET
Good night.
Go to bed and get some sleep - you'll need it.

Exeunt LADY CAPULET and Nurse

JULIET
Goodbye! I don't know if we'll ever meet again.
I can feel a faint chill running through my veins
That almost seems to freeze my heart.
I'll ask them to come back again to comfort me.
Nurse! But what could she do to help?
The horrible deed I have to do I must do on my own.
Here is the bottle.
What if this mixture doesn't work?
Will I have to get married tomorrow morning?
No, no - this dagger will prevent that. I'll keep it here.

Laying down her dagger

What if it be a poison which the Friar
Subtly hath ministered to have me dead,
Lest in this marriage he should be dishonoured,
Because he married me before to Romeo?
I fear it is, and yet methinks it should not,
For he hath still been tried a holy man.
How if, when I am laid into the tomb,
I wake before the time that Romeo
Come to redeem me? There's a fearful point!
Shall I not then be stifled in the vault,
To whose foul mouth no healthsome air breathes in,
And there die strangled ere my Romeo comes?
Or if I live, is it not very like
The horrible conceit of death and night,
Together with the terror of the place -
As in a vault, an ancient receptacle,
Where for these many hundred years the bones
Of all my buried ancestors are packed,
Where bloody Tybalt, yet but green in earth,
Lies fest'ring in his shroud, where, as they say,
At some hours in the night spirits resort -
Alack, alack, is it not like that I,
So early waking - what with loathsome smells,
And shrieks like mandrakes' torn out of the earth,
That living mortals, hearing them, run mad -
O, if I wake, shall I not be distraught,
Environéd with all these hideous fears,
And madly play with my forefathers' joints,
And pluck the mangled Tybalt from his shroud,
And in this rage, with some great kinsman's bone,
As with a club, dash out my desp'rate brains?
O, look! methinks I see my cousin's ghost
Seeking out Romeo that did spit his body
Upon a rapier's point. Stay, Tybalt, stay!
Romeo, Romeo, Romeo! Here's drink - I drink to thee.

She falls upon her bed, within the curtains

What if it's a poison which the Friar
Has secretly given me to kill me
In case my remarriage disgraces him
Because he already married me to Romeo?
I'm worried it is poison. And yet I don't think it would be
Because he has been proven to be a holy man.
What if, when I am laid in the tomb,
I wake up before Romeo
Arrives to collect me? That's a terrible thought!
Wouldn't I then be trapped in the tomb
Where there is nothing but foul air to breathe
And I'll die of suffocation before Romeo arrives?
Or, if I live, I'll be left to face,
The unpleasantness of death and darkness,
As well as the general horror of a place
Like a crypt - an old building -
Where, for many hundreds of years, the bones
Of all my ancestors have been buried.
Where Tybalt, only recently deceased,
Lies decaying in his coffin. Where, it's said,
Sometimes at night ghosts are found.
Oh dear, oh dear. Isn't it likely that I -
If I wake up early, with the horrible smells
And ghostly shrieks of the dead
That the living run mad from hearing them -
Oh, if I wake up early, won't I be driven mad,
Surrounded by all these horrible things?
And start playing with my ancestors' bones?
And take Tybalt's body out of its coffin?
And, in this mad state, with one of my cousin's bones,
Using it like a club, bash my own brains out?
Look! I think I can see Tybalt's ghost
Looking for Romeo that stabbed his body
With the point of his sword. No, Tybalt, no!
Romeo. Oh, Romeo, Romeo! I drink this for you.

She falls upon her bed, within the curtains

ACT IV SCENE IV. Hall in Capulet's house.

Enter LADY CAPULET and Nurse

LADY CAPULET
Hold, take these keys and fetch more spices, Nurse.

NURSE
They call for dates and quinces in the pastry.

Enter CAPULET

CAPULET
Come, stir, stir, stir! the second cock hath crowed,
The curfew bell hath rung, 'tis three a'clock:
Look to the baked meats, good Angelica,
Spare not for the cost.

NURSE
Go, you cot-quean, go,
Get you to bed. Faith, you'll be sick tomorrow
For this night's watching.

CAPULET
No, not a whit. What, I have watched ere now
All night for lesser cause, and ne'er been sick.

LADY CAPULET
Ay, you have been a mouse-hunt in your time,
But I will watch you from such watching now.

Exeunt LADY CAPULET and Nurse

CAPULET
A jealous hood, a jealous hood!

Enter three or four Servingmen, with spits, logs, and baskets

Now, fellow,
What is there?

First Servant
Things for the cook, sir, but I know not what.

ACT IV SCENE IV. Hall in Capulet's house.

Enter LADY CAPULET and Nurse

LADY CAPULET
Wait, take these keys and fetch more spices, Nurse.

NURSE
They've asked for dates and pears in the kitchen.

Enter CAPULET

CAPULET
Come on, get going! The cock's already crowed twice,
The morning bell has rung - it's three o'clock already.
Don't forget the meat, please, Angelica.
Don't worry about the cost.

NURSE
Look at you go.
You should get to bed or you'll be sick tomorrow
From staying up so late.

CAPULET
No, not at all. I've stayed up before
All night for less important things and not been sick.

LADY CAPULET
Yes, you were quite the ladies man in your time.
But I'll make sure you don't do it again.

Exeunt LADY CAPULET and Nurse

CAPULET
She's just jealous. Jealous!

Enter three or four Servingmen, with spits, logs, and baskets

Hey you,
What have you got there?

First Servant
Stuff for the cook, sir. But I don't know what.

CAPULET
Make haste, make haste.

Exit First Servant

Sirrah, fetch drier logs.
Call Peter, he will show thee where they are.

Second Servant
I have a head, sir, that will find out logs,
And never trouble Peter for the matter.

Exit

CAPULET
Mass, and well said, a merry whoreson, ha!
Thou shalt be loggerhead. Good faith, 'tis day.
The County will be here with music straight,
For so he said he would. I hear him near.

Music within

Nurse! Wife! What ho! What, Nurse, I say!

Re-enter Nurse

Go waken Juliet, go and trim her up,
I'll go and chat with Paris. Hie, make haste,
Make haste, the bridegroom he is come already,
Make haste, I say.

Exeunt

CAPULET
Well, go on. Go on.

Exit First Servant

You - fetch better wood.
Ask Peter - he'll show you where it is.

Second Servant
I am able, sir, to find where it is
Without asking Peter for help.

Exit

CAPULET
Goodness, well said, you cheeky young man, you, ha ha!
You'll be trouble. Goodness - it's morning.
Paris will be here with musicians soon
He said he would. And I can hear him coming.

Music within

Nurse! Wife! Hello! Oi, Nurse!

Re-enter Nurse

Go and wake up Juliet. Go and get her ready.
I'll go and talk to Paris. Go on, quick,
Quick! Her husband-to-be is here already.
Quick, I said.

Exeunt

ACT IV SCENE V. Juliet's chamber.

Enter Nurse

NURSE
Mistress, what, mistress! Juliet! Fast, I warrant her, she.
Why, lamb! why, lady! fie, you slug-a-bed!
Why, love, I say! madam! Sweet heart! why, bride!
What, not a word? you take your pennyworths now;
Sleep for a week, for the next night I warrant,
The County Paris hath set up his rest
That you shall rest but little. God forgive me!
Marry and amen! How sound is she asleep!
I must needs wake her. Madam, madam, madam!
Ay, let the County take you in your bed;
He'll fright you up, i'faith. Will it not be?

Undraws the curtains

What, dressed, and in your clothes, and down again!
I must needs wake you. Lady! lady! lady!
Alas, alas! Help, help! my lady's dead!
O weraday that ever I was born!
Some aqua-vitae, ho! My lord! my lady!

Enter LADY CAPULET

LADY CAPULET
What noise is here?

NURSE
O lamentable day!

LADY CAPULET
What is the matter?

NURSE
Look, look! O heavy day!

LADY CAPULET
O me, O me, my child, my only life!
Revive, look up, or I will die with thee.
Help, help! Call help.

ACT IV SCENE V. Juliet's chamber.

Enter Nurse

NURSE
Juliet! Oh, Juliet! Juliet! Fast asleep, I'll bet.
Oh, darling! My lady! Goodness, what a sleepyhead!
Darling! Juliet! Sweetheart! Oh, bride-to-be!
What, nothing? You should get your forty winks now.
Sleep for a week. Because tonight, I'll bet,
Paris has planned,
That you won't get any sleep. God forgive me,
But it's true. She's sound asleep!
I must wake her up. Juliet. Juliet. Juliet!
I should let Paris take you in your bed.
That would wake you up, I'll bet. Wouldn't it?

Undraws the curtains

What, dressed in your best clothes! And gone back to bed?
I must wake you up. Juliet! Juliet! Juliet!
Oh no! Oh no! Help! help! Juliet's dead!
Oh, curse the day I was born!
Someone get me a drink! Quick! Sir! Madam!

Enter LADY CAPULET

LADY CAPULET
What's all this noise?

NURSE
Oh, what a terrible day!

LADY CAPULET
What's the matter?

NURSE
Look! Look! Oh, it's such a sad day!

LADY CAPULET
Oh my! Oh my! My child, my reason for living!
Wake up. Look at me. Or I might as well be dead too.
Help! Help! Call for help.

Enter CAPULET

CAPULET
For shame, bring Juliet forth, her lord is come.

NURSE
She's dead, deceased, she's dead, alack the day!

LADY CAPULET
Alack the day, she's dead, she's dead, she's dead!

CAPULET
Hah, let me see her. Out, alas! she's cold.
Her blood is settled, and her joints are stiff:
Life and these lips have long been separated;
Death lies on her like an untimely frost
Upon the sweetest flower of all the field.

NURSE
O lamentable day!

LADY CAPULET
O woeful time!

CAPULET
Death that hath tane her hence to make me wail
Ties up my tongue and will not let me speak.

Enter FRIAR LAWRENCE and PARIS, with Musicians

FRIAR LAWRENCE
Come, is the bride ready to go to church?

CAPULET
Ready to go, but never to return. -
O son, the night before thy wedding day
Hath Death lain with thy wife. There she lies,
Flower as she was, deflowered by him.
Death is my son-in-law, Death is my heir,
My daughter he hath wedded. I will die,
And leave him all; life, living, all is Death's.

PARIS
Have I thought long to see this morning's face,
And doth it give me such a sight as this?

Enter CAPULET

CAPULET
Shame on you. Bring Juliet out - her husband's here.

NURSE
She's dead, gone, dead! Oh, what a horrible day!

LADY CAPULET
A terrible day. She's dead, she's dead, she's dead!

CAPULET
What! Let me see her. Oh no! She's cold.
There's no pulse. And she's stiff.
Life has long since left these lips.
Death makes her look like she's covered in frost.
She was the sweetest girl in the world.

NURSE
Oh, what a terrible day!

LADY CAPULET
Oh, how awful!

CAPULET
Her death, which has given me reason to cry,
Has also left me speechless.

Enter FRIAR LAWRENCE and PARIS, with Musicians

FRIAR LAWRENCE
Come on then, is the bride ready to go to church?

CAPULET
She'll go but only to be buried.
Oh, Paris! The night before her wedding day
Death has taken your wife-to-be. There she is -
Angel that she was - stolen by death.
Because death has taken her, I will have no heir.
Death has taken my daughter and, when I die,
I'll have no-one to leave everything to - all lost to death.

PARIS
I've waited for this day for such a long time.
And this is what greets me?

LADY CAPULET
Accursed, unhappy, wretched, hateful day!
Most miserable hour that e'er time saw
In lasting labour of his pilgrimage!
But one, poor one, one poor and loving child,
But one thing to rejoice and solace in,
And cruel death hath catched it from my sight!

NURSE
O woe! O woeful, woeful, woeful day!
Most lamentable day, most woeful day
That ever, ever, I did yet behold!
O day, O day, O day, O hateful day!
Never was seen so black a day as this.
O woeful day, O woeful day!

PARIS
Beguiled, divorced, wrongéd, spited, slain!
Most detestable Death, by thee beguiled,
By cruel, cruel thee quite overthrown!
O love! O life! not life, but love in death!

CAPULET
Despised, distresséd, hated, martyred, killed!
Uncomfortable time, why cam'st thou now
To murder, murder our solemnity?
O child, O child! my soul, and not my child!
Dead art thou. Alack, my child is dead,
And with my child my joys are buriéd.

FRIAR LAWRENCE
Peace ho, for shame! confusion's cure lives not
In these confusions. Heaven and yourself
Had part in this fair maid, now heaven hath all,
And all the better is it for the maid:
Your part in her you could not keep from death,
But heaven keeps his part in eternal life.
The most you sought was her promotion,
For 'twas your heaven she should be advanced,
And weep ye now, seeing she is advanced
Above the clouds, as high as heaven itself?
O, in this love, you love your child so ill
That you run mad, seeing that she is well.

LADY CAPULET
What a terrible, unhappy, awful, horrible day!
The most miserable day ever
Since time began!
I had one, just one, one poor, darling child.
Just one thing to rejoice and take solace in.
And death has snatched her from me!

NURSE
Oh, how terrible! What a terrible, terrible, terrible day!
A tragic day. The most terrible day
That I ever, ever, saw!
Today! Yes, today! Oh, today has been a horrible day!
There's never been a day as bad as this.
Oh, what a terrible day, a terrible day!

PARIS
I've been cheated, foiled, wronged, denied, defeated!
Cruel death has beaten me.
It has utterly defeated me!
Oh, my love! My life! No, not life - my love is dead!

CAPULET
Hated, distraught, unloved, dead and gone!
What horrible timing. Why is it now
That this terrible thing has happened to spoil everything?
Oh, my child! My poor child! Take me and not my child!
You are dead! Oh no! My child is dead.
And with my child I've lost all reason for happiness.

FRIAR LAWRENCE
Wait, please. Goodness me! You won't find solace
If you keep on like this. God gave you
This child. And now God's taken her back.
And that's a good thing for her.
You wouldn't have been able to stop her dying
But now in heaven she'll live forever.
The most you wanted was for her to get on in life -
It was your dream that she should do well.
And now you're crying because she's reached
So high as to reach heaven itself?
By doing this, it suggests you don't love your child at all
If you're upset that she's done so well.

She's not well married that lives married long,
But she's best married that dies married young.
Dry up your tears, and stick your rosemary
On this fair corse, and, as the custom is,
In all her best array bear her to church;
For though fond nature bids us all lament,
Yet nature's tears are reason's merriment.

CAPULET
All things that we ordainéd festival,
Turn from their office to black funeral:
Our instruments to melancholy bells,
Our wedding cheer to a sad burial feast;
Our solemn hymns to sullen dirges change;
Our bridal flowers serve for a buried corse;
And all things change them to the contrary.

FRIAR LAWRENCE
Sir, go you in, and, madam, go with him;
And go, Sir Paris. every one prepare
To follow this fair corse unto her grave.
The heavens do low'r upon you for some ill;
Move them no more by crossing their high will.

Exeunt CAPULET, LADY CAPULET, PARIS, and FRIAR LAWRENCE

First Musician
Faith, we may put up our pipes and be gone.

NURSE
Honest good fellows, ah put up, put up,
For well you know this is a pitiful case.

Exit

First Musician
Ay, by my troth, the case may be amended.

Enter PETER

PETER
Musicians, O, musicians, 'Heart's ease', 'Heart's
ease'! O, and you will have me live, play 'Heart's ease'.

Someone who's married for a long time isn't better off
Than someone who marries and dies young.
So stop crying and prepare what is necessary
For what has happened. And, as is the custom,
Take her to church in her best clothes.
Because, although our emotions tell us to mourn,
Yet her fate gives us reason to be cheerful.

CAPULET
All the brightly coloured things we ordered,
Will now be used for her funeral.
Cheerful instruments become funeral bells.
Our wedding feast becomes a wake.
Our wedding hymns become sad funeral songs.
Our bridal bouquets will be laid with her corpse.
Everything becomes opposite to what it's supposed to be.

FRIAR LAWRENCE
Sir, please go in. And, you too, madam.
And you, Paris. Everyone get ready
To take poor Juliet to be buried.
You might think God has cursed you
But don't anger him by questioning his will.

Exeunt CAPULET, LADY CAPULET, PARIS, and FRIAR LAWRENCE

First Musician
Yes, we will put away our instruments and go.

NURSE
Yes, gentlemen, put them away, put them away.
You can tell this is a very sad time.

Exit

First Musician
Yes, but I hope that soon changes.

Enter PETER

PETER
Musicians, oh, musicians. 'Heart's ease', 'Heart's
ease'. If you want to help me, play 'Heart's ease'.

First Musician
Why 'Heart's ease'?

PETER
O musicians, because my heart itself plays 'My
heart is full'. O play me some merry dump
to comfort me.

First Musician
Not a dump we, 'tis no time to play now.

PETER
You will not then?

First Musician
No.

PETER
I will then give it you soundly.

First Musician
What will you give us?

PETER
No money, on my faith, but the gleek;
I will give you the minstrel.

First Musician
Then I will give you the serving-creature.

PETER
Then will I lay the serving-creature's dagger on
your pate. I will carry no crotchets, I'll re you,
I'll fa you. Do you note me?

First Musician
And you re us and fa us, you note us.

Second Musician
Pray you put up your dagger, and put out your wit.

First Musician
Why 'Heart's ease'?

PETER
Oh, musicians, because my heart itself is so
full of sorrow. Please play me a cheerful but sad tune,
to comfort me.

First Musician
No, we won't. It's not the right time to play now.

PETER
You won't?

First Musician
No.

PETER
In that case I've this for you.

First Musician
What?

PETER
No money - no fear - but the finger.
You're poor minstrels.

First Musician
And you're a servant.

PETER
Then I'll use my servant's knife on
your head. I won't hesitate. I'll have you,
I'll beat you. Are you listening?

First Musician
If you have us and beat us, you'll hear us.

Second Musician
Go on - use your knife. It's sharper than your wit.

PETER
Then have at you with my wit! I will dry-beat you
with an iron wit, and put up my iron dagger. Answer
me like men:
'When griping grief the heart doth wound,
And doleful dumps the mind oppress,
Then music with her silver sound -'
Why 'silver sound'? why 'music with her silver
sound'? What say you, Simon Catling?

Musician
Marry, sir, because silver hath a sweet sound.

PETER
Prates! What say you, Hugh Rebeck?

Second Musician
I say 'silver sound,' because musicians sound for silver.

PETER
Prates too! What say you, James Soundpost?

Third Musician
Faith, I know not what to say.

PETER
O, I cry you mercy, you are the singer; I will say
for you: It is 'music with her silver sound'
because musicians have no gold for sounding.
'Then music with her silver sound
With speedy help doth lend redress.'

Exit

First Musician
What a pestilent knave is this same!

Second Musician
Hang him, Jack! Come, we'll in here, tarry for the
mourners, and stay dinner.

Exeunt

PETER
Then I'll beat you with my wit! I will beat you
with my iron-strong wit rather than my metal knife. Tell
me, if you're men:
'When terrible grief wounds the heart,
And miserable songs overcome the mind,
Then music with a silver sound...'
Why 'silver sound'? Why is it 'music with a silver
sound'? What do you think, Simon the lute player?

Musician
Because, sir, 'silver' has a sweet sound.

PETER
Terrible! What about you, Hugh the lyre player?

Second Musician
I think it's 'silver sound' because musicians play for silver.

PETER
Also terrible! What about you, James the violin player?

Third Musician
Honestly, I don't know what to say.

PETER
Oh, forgive me – you're the singer. I will say
it for you. It is 'music with a silver sound,'
because musicians have no silver themselves.
'Then music with her silver sound
With speedily help their sorrows rewind.'

Exit

First Musician
What an annoying man he is!

Second Musician
To hell with him! Come on, we'll go in here, wait for the
mourners, and stay for dinner.

Exeunt

ACT V SCENE I. Mantua. A street.

Enter ROMEO

ROMEO
If I may trust the flattering truth of sleep,
My dreams presage some joyful news at hand.
My bosom's lord sits lightly in his throne,
And all this day an unaccustomed spirit
Lifts me above the ground with cheerful thoughts.
I dreamt my lady came and found me dead
Strange dream, that gives a dead man leave
to think!
And breathed such life with kisses in my lips,
That I revived and was an emperor.
Ah me, how sweet is love itself possessed,
When but love's shadows are so rich in joy!

Enter BALTHASAR, booted

News from Verona! How now, Balthasar?
Dost thou not bring me letters from the Friar?
How doth my lady? Is my father well?
How fares my Juliet? That I ask again;
For nothing can be ill if she be well.

BALTHASAR
Then she is well and nothing can be ill:
Her body sleeps in Capels' monument,
And her immortal part with angels lives.
I saw her laid low in her kindred's vault,
And presently took post to tell it you.
O pardon me for bringing these ill news,
Since you did leave it for my office, sir.

ROMEO
Is it e'en so? then I defy you, stars!
Thou knowest my lodging, get me ink and paper,
And hire post-horses; I will hence tonight.

BALTHASAR
I do beseech you, sir, have patience:
Your looks are pale and wild, and do import
Some misadventure.

ACT V SCENE I. Mantua. A street.

Enter ROMEO

ROMEO
If I believe what I saw in my sleep,
My dreams predict some happy news is coming.
My heart feels very light
And all day an unfamiliar feeling
Has lifted my spirits with happy thoughts.
I dreamt Juliet came and found me dead -
Strange that a dream gives a dead man the ability
to think -
And breathed so much life into my lips with kisses
That I was revived and felt like an emperor.
Ah! How sweet love can be,
When even thoughts of it bring such joy!

Enter BALTHASAR, booted

It's my friend from Verona! How are you, Balthasar?
Have you brought me some letters from the Friar?
How is my wife? Is my father well?
How is Juliet? I'll ask that again.
Because nothing can be wrong if she is alright.

BALTHASAR
Then if she is alright nothing can be wrong.
But her body lies in the Capulet tomb
And her immortal soul is with the angels.
I saw her laid to rest in her family's crypt
And immediately came here to tell you.
Please forgive me for bringing you such sad news
But it's what you asked me to do, sir.

ROMEO
Can it be true? Then to hell with everything!
You know where I live. Get me pen and paper
And hire some horses - I will leave here tonight.

BALTHASAR
Please, sir, be patient.
You look pale and unsettled, which suggests
You're going to do something foolish.

ROMEO
Tush, thou art deceived.
Leave me, and do the thing I bid thee do.
Hast thou no letters to me from the Friar?

BALTHASAR
No, my good lord.

ROMEO
No matter, get thee gone,
And hire those horses; I'll be with thee straight.

Exit BALTHASAR

Well, Juliet, I will lie with thee tonight.
Let's see for means. O mischief, thou art swift
To enter in the thoughts of desperate men!
I do remember an apothecary,
And hereabouts 'a dwells, which late I noted
In tattered weeds, with overwhelming brows,
Culling of simples; meagre were his looks,
Sharp misery had worn him to the bones;
And in his needy shop a tortoise hung,
An alligator stuffed, and other skins
Of ill-shaped fishes, and about his shelves
A beggarly account of empty boxes,
Green earthen pots, bladders and musty seeds,
Remnants of packthread, and old cakes of roses,
Were thinly scattered, to make up a show.
Noting this penury, to myself I said,
'And if a man did need a poison now,
Whose sale is present death in Mantua,
Here lives a caitiff wretch would sell it him.'
O this same thought did but forerun my need,
And this same needy man must sell it me.
As I remember, this should be the house.
Being holiday, the beggar's shop is shut.
What ho, apothecary!

Enter Apothecary

APOTHECARY
Who calls so loud?

ROMEO
No, you're wrong.
Now leave me. Go and do the thing I asked you to do.
Has the Friar not given you any letters for me?

BALTHASAR
No, sir.

ROMEO
Never mind. Go
And get those horses. I'll be with you soon.

Exit BALTHASAR

Juliet, I will join you tonight.
Now how shall I do it? Terrible thoughts are quick
To enter the minds of desperate men.
I remember a chemist
That lives nearby - who I recently saw
In tatty clothing with thick eyebrows
Picking herbs for remedies. He didn't look very well -
Hard times had led to him becoming skin and bones.
And in his sparse shop hung a tortoise,
A stuffed alligator, and other skins
Of odd-looking fishes. On his shelves
Were a small account of empty boxes,
Green clay pots, bottles and old seeds.
Scraps of twine and old petals of roses
Were thinly scattered to make it look nice.
Noting his poverty, I said to myself that
If a man needed poison -
The sale of which is punishable by death in Mantua -
This is the poor pathetic man who would sell it to him.
This thought foreshadowed my need
And this same desperate man must sell me some.
If I remember correctly, this is his house.
As it's a holiday, his little shop is shut.
Hello! Mr Chemist!

Enter Apothecary

APOTHECARY
Who's that?

ROMEO
Come hither, man. I see that thou art poor.
Hold, there is forty ducats; let me have
A dram of poison, such soon-speeding gear
As will disperse itself through all the veins,
That the life-weary taker may fall dead,
And that the trunk may be discharged of breath
As violently as hasty powder fired
Doth hurry from the fatal cannon's womb.

APOTHECARY
Such mortal drugs I have, but Mantua's law
Is death to any he that utters them.

ROMEO
Art thou so bare and full of wretchedness,
And fearest to die? Famine is in thy cheeks,
Need and oppression starveth in thy eyes,
Contempt and beggary hangs upon thy back;
The world is not thy friend, nor the world's law;
The world affords no law to make thee rich;
Then be not poor, but break it and take this.

APOTHECARY
My poverty, but not my will, consents.

ROMEO
I pay thy poverty, and not thy will.

APOTHECARY
Put this in any liquid thing you will
And drink it off, and if you had the strength
Of twenty men, it would dispatch you straight.

ROMEO
There is thy gold, worse poison to men's souls,
Doing more murder in this loathsome world,
Than these poor compounds that thou mayst not sell.
I sell thee poison, thou hast sold me none.
Farewell, buy food, and get thyself in flesh.
Come, cordial and not poison, go with me
To Juliet's grave, for there must I use thee.

Exeunt

ROMEO
Come here, you. I can see you're poor
So here is forty gold coins. Give me
A dose of poison - something fast-acting -
That will spread itself through my body
So that I, who am weary of life, will die
And my body will breathe its last
As quick as a cannonball is fired
From the mouth of a cannon.

APOTHECARY
I have poisons like that but according to the law
I would be sentenced to death if I sold them.

ROMEO
Really? Someone as poor and wretched as you
Is afraid of death? You look half-starved.
I can desperation and suffering in your eyes.
Rejection and poverty weigh you down.
The world has not been kind to you and neither is the law.
The world doesn't allow you to be rich.
But don't be poor - break the law and take this money.

APOTHECARY
My desperation makes me agree but I am still unwilling.

ROMEO
In that case, I'll pay your desperation and not your will.

APOTHECARY
Put this in any liquid you want
And drink it all and, even if you had the strength
Of twenty men, it would kill you instantly.

ROMEO
Here's your money, which does more harm than poison
As it leads to more murders in this horrible world
Than these potions that you're not allowed to sell.
I'm the one giving you poison - you haven't given me any.
Goodbye. Go buy food - put some meat on your bones.
This is sweet juice and not poison that I will take with me
To Juliet's grave. For that's where I must use it.

Exeunt

ACT V SCENE II. Friar Lawrence's cell.

Enter FRIAR JOHN

FRIAR JOHN
Holy Franciscan Friar! brother, ho!

Enter FRIAR LAWRENCE

FRIAR LAWRENCE
This same should be the voice of Friar John.
Welcome from Mantua. What says Romeo?
Or, if his mind be writ, give me his letter.

FRIAR JOHN
Going to find a barefoot brother out
One of our order, to associate me,
Here in this city visiting the sick,
And finding him, the searchers of the town,
Suspecting that we both were in a house
Where the infectious pestilence did reign,
Sealed up the doors, and would not let us forth,
So that my speed to Mantua there was stayed.

FRIAR LAWRENCE
Who bare my letter then to Romeo?

FRIAR JOHN
I could not send it - here it is again -
Nor get a messenger to bring it thee,
So fearful were they of infection.

FRIAR LAWRENCE
Unhappy fortune! By my brotherhood,
The letter was not nice but full of charge
Of dear import, and the neglecting it
May do much danger. Friar John, go hence,
Get me an iron crow and bring it straight
Unto my cell.

FRIAR JOHN
Brother, I'll go and bring it thee.

Exit

ACT V SCENE II. Friar Lawrence's cell.

Enter FRIAR JOHN

FRIAR JOHN
Hello! Friar Lawrence! Friar? Hello!

Enter FRIAR LAWRENCE

FRIAR LAWRENCE
That sounds like Friar John's voice.
Welcome back from Mantua. What did Romeo say?
Or, if he wrote down his thoughts, give me his letter.

FRIAR JOHN
I went to find a fellow Friar -
Someone of our faith - to accompany me
Who was here in this city visiting the sick.
And, when I found him, the guards of the town -
Believing that we were in a house
Where the plague had been known to be -
Sealed the doors and would not let us out
So my journey to Mantua was delayed.

FRIAR LAWRENCE
Then who took my letter to Romeo?

FRIAR JOHN
I couldn't take it - here it is -
Nor could I get a messenger to send it to you -
They were so afraid of infection.

FRIAR LAWRENCE
Oh, no! Friar John,
The letter was not trivial but was full of news
That was very important and failing to deliver it
May have caused many problems. Friar John, go and
Get me an iron crowbar and bring it straight
To my church.

FRIAR JOHN
I'll go and get it now.

Exit

FRIAR LAWRENCE
Now must I to the monument alone,
Within three hours will fair Juliet wake.
She will beshrew me much that Romeo
Hath had no notice of these accidents;
But I will write again to Mantua,
And keep her at my cell till Romeo come,
Poor living corse, closed in a dead man's tomb!

Exit

FRIAR LAWRENCE
Now I must go to the tomb on my own.
Within three hours Juliet will wake up.
She will blame me for Romeo
Not having been told of our plans.
I will write again to him in Mantua
And keep her at my church until Romeo comes.
Poor thing - trapped in a tomb!

Exit

ACT V SCENE III. A churchyard; in it a tomb belonging to the Capulets.

Enter PARIS, and his Page bearing flowers and a torch

PARIS
Give me thy torch, boy. Hence, and stand aloof.
Yet put it out, for I would not be seen.
Under yond yew-trees lay thee all along,
Holding thine ear close to the hollow ground,
So shall no foot upon the churchyard tread,
Being loose, unfirm with digging up of graves,
But thou shalt hear it. Whistle then to me
As signal that thou hear'st something approach.
Give me those flowers. Do as I bid thee, go.

PAGE
[Aside] I am almost afraid to stand alone
Here in the churchyard, yet I will adventure.

Retires

PARIS
Sweet flower, with flowers thy bridal bed I strew -
O woe, thy canopy is dust and stones! -
Which with sweet water nightly I will dew,
Or wanting that, with tears distilled by moans.
The obsequies that I for thee will keep
Nightly shall be to strew thy grave and weep.

The Page whistles

The boy gives warning, something doth approach.
What cursed foot wanders this way tonight,
To cross my obsequies and true love's rite?
What, with a torch! Muffle me, night, a while.

Retires

Enter ROMEO and BALTHASAR, with a torch, mattock, & c

ROMEO
Give me that mattock and the wrenching iron.
Hold, take this letter; early in the morning
See thou deliver it to my lord and father.
Give me the light. Upon thy life I charge thee,
What e'er thou hear'st or seest, stand all aloof,

ACT V SCENE III. A churchyard; in it a tomb belonging to the Capulets.

Enter PARIS, and his Page bearing flowers and a torch

PARIS
Give me your torch, boy. Go stand a short distance away.
Actually, put it out - I don't want to be seen.
Under those yew trees lie down and wait.
Keep your ear close to the ground
So no-one will be able to enter the churchyard -
The ground of which is loose from graves being dug -
Without you hearing it. Whistle to me,
As a signal when you can hear someone approaching.
Give me those flowers. Do as I said, go.

PAGE
[Aside] I am afraid to stand on my own
In the churchyard. But I will do it.

Retires

PARIS
Darling Juliet, I'll adorn your bed with flowers -
Oh dear! You are covered in dust and stones -
And I'll freshen them every night with sweet water.
Or, failing that, with tears caused by my misery.
The duty that I will do for you
Will be to tidy your grave and cry over you every night.

The Page whistles

The boy's giving me a warning someone's coming.
Who could possibly be coming here tonight,
To interrupt the duty I must perform for my love?
And they have a torch! I'll let the darkness hide me.

Retires

Enter ROMEO and BALTHASAR, with a torch, mattock, & c

ROMEO
Give me that pickaxe and the crowbar.
Good. Take this letter and early in the morning
Make sure you deliver it to my father.
Give me the torch and swear to me,
Whatever you hear or see, you'll stay away

And do not interrupt me in my course.
Why I descend into this bed of death
Is partly to behold my lady's face,
But chiefly to take thence from her dead finger
A precious ring, a ring that I must use
In dear employment; therefore hence, be gone.
But if thou, jealous, dost return to pry
In what I further shall intend to do,
By heaven, I will tear thee joint by joint,
And strew this hungry churchyard with thy limbs.
The time and my intents are savage-wild,
More fierce and more inexorable far
Than empty tigers or the roaring sea.

BALTHASAR
I will be gone, sir, and not trouble ye.

ROMEO
So shalt thou show me friendship. Take thou that,
Live and be prosperous, and farewell, good fellow.

BALTHASAR
[Aside] For all this same, I'll hide me hereabout,
His looks I fear, and his intents I doubt.

Retires

ROMEO
Thou detestable maw, thou womb of death,
Gorged with the dearest morsel of the earth,
Thus I enforce thy rotten jaws to open,
And in despite I'll cram thee with more food.

Opens the tomb

PARIS
This is that banished haughty Montague,
That murdered my love's cousin, with which grief
It is supposèd the fair creature died,
And here is come to do some villainous shame
To the dead bodies. I will apprehend him.

Comes forward

And not interrupt me in what I do.
The reason I'm going into this tomb
Is partly to see Juliet's face
But mainly to take off her dead finger
A precious ring - a ring that I must use
For something important. So go on. Go now.
If you suspect something and come back to spy on
What else I intend to do,
I swear, I will tear you limb from limb
And strew your body parts around this churchyard.
It's late and my mood is dark.
It's angrier and more relentless
Than hungry tigers or the stormy sea.

BALTHASAR
I will go, sir, and I won't bother you.

ROMEO
And that'll prove you're my friend. Take this.
I hope you have a long, prosperous life. Goodbye, friend.

BALTHASAR
[Aside] In spite of what I said, I'll hide nearby.
He looks odd. I'm worried about what he intends to do.

Retires

ROMEO
This is a horrible door to a place of death,
Which has engulfed the most beautiful woman on earth.
I will force the door to open
And, in my misery, I'll put more inside!

Opens the tomb

PARIS
That's Romeo who was banished
For murdering Juliet's cousin - from the grief of which
She is believed to have died.
And he's come here to do something terribly disrespectful
To the dead bodies. I will arrest him.

Comes forward

Stop thy unhallowed toil, vile Montague!
Can vengeance be pursued further than death?
Condemned villain, I do apprehend thee.
Obey and go with me, for thou must die.

ROMEO
I must indeed, and therefore came I hither.
Good gentle youth, tempt not a desp'rate man,
Fly hence, and leave me. Think upon these gone,
Let them affright thee. I beseech thee, youth,
Put not another sin upon my head,
By urging me to fury: O be gone!
By heaven, I love thee better than myself,
For I come hither armed against myself:
Stay not, be gone; live, and hereafter say,
A madman's mercy bade thee run away.

PARIS
I do defy thy conjuration,
And apprehend thee for a felon here.

ROMEO
Wilt thou provoke me? then have at thee, boy!

They fight

PAGE
O Lord, they fight! I will go call the Watch.

Exit

PARIS
O, I am slain!

Falls

If thou be merciful,
Open the tomb, lay me with Juliet.

Dies

ROMEO
In faith, I will. Let me peruse this face.
Mercutio's kinsman, noble County Paris!
What said my man, when my betosséd soul
Did not attend him as we rode? I think

Stop what you're doing, Romeo Montague!
What more could you do besides kill them?
You're a wanted man and I hereby arrest you.
Do as I say and come with me. Because you must die.

ROMEO
Yes, I must. And that's why I came here.
Please sir, don't push me.
Go away, leave me alone. Think about these dead people -
Let them scare you. I beg you, sir,
Don't cause yourself more trouble
By making me angry. Go away!
I swear, I care about you more than I care about myself
Because I've come here planning to do harm to myself.
Don't wait. Go. Live. And afterwards you'll say
A madman in his mercy told you to run away.

PARIS
I refuse your suggestions,
And arrest you for your crimes.

ROMEO
You still want to provoke me? Then take this, you!

They fight

PAGE
Oh, God, they're fighting! I'll go and get the guards.

Exit

PARIS
Oh, I've been killed!

Falls

If you are merciful,
Then open the tomb and lay me beside Juliet.

Dies

ROMEO
Alright, I will. Let me just see your face.
It's Mercutio's cousin - Count Paris!
What did my friend say? My troubled soul
Didn't listen to him as we travelled? I think

He told me Paris should have married Juliet.
Said he not so? or did I dream it so?
Or am I mad, hearing him talk of Juliet,
To think it was so? O give me thy hand,
One writ with me in sour misfortune's book!
I'll bury thee in a triumphant grave.
A grave? O no, a lantern, slaughtered youth;
For here lies Juliet, and her beauty makes
This vault a feasting presence full of light.
Death, lie thou there, by a dead man interred.

Laying PARIS in the tomb

How oft when men are at the point of death
Have they been merry, which their keepers call
A light'ning before death! O how may I
Call this a light'ning? O my love, my wife,
Death, that hath sucked the honey of thy breath,
Hath had no power yet upon thy beauty:
Thou art not conquered, beauty's ensign yet
Is crimson in thy lips and in thy cheeks,
And Death's pale flag is not advanced there.
Tybalt, liest thou there in thy bloody sheet?
O, what more favour can I do to thee,
Than with that hand that cut thy youth in twain
To sunder his that was thine enemy?
Forgive me, cousin. Ah, dear Juliet,
Why art thou yet so fair? Shall I believe
That unsubstantial Death is amorous,
And that the lean abhorred monster keeps
Thee here in dark to be his paramour?
For fear of that, I still will stay with thee,
And never from this palace of dim night
Depart again. Here, here will I remain
With worms that are thy chamber-maids; O here
Will I set up my everlasting rest,
And shake the yoke of inauspicious stars
From this world-wearied flesh. Eyes, look your last!
Arms, take your last embrace! and, lips, O you
The doors of breath, seal with a righteous kiss
A dateless bargain to engrossing death!

He told me Paris was to marry Juliet.
Did he say that? Or did I dream it?
Or am I mad, having heard him talk of Juliet,
That I think it was that? Oh, give me your hand -
To which I caused misfortune to happen!
I'll bury you in a magnificent grave.
A grave? No it's a palace, poor Paris,
Because here is Juliet and her beauty makes
This tomb seem to be a wonderful place full of light.
Death belongs with Paris - killed by a man about to die.

Laying PARIS in the tomb

When prisoners have been at the point of death,
They've often been merry. Which the gaolers call
Feeling lighter before death. But how could I
Call this 'feeling lighter'? Oh, my love! My wife!
Death, that has taken away your sweet breath,
Has not yet had any effect on your beauty.
Death hasn't won you yet. Your beauty can still be seen
In the red of your lips and in your cheeks.
Death has not made them pale.
Tybalt, is that you in that bloody sheet?
What more could I do for you
Than, with the hand that cut you down,
To kill the man that was your enemy?
Forgive me, Tybalt! Ah, dear Juliet,
Why are you still so beautiful? Can I believe
That death is weak and has feelings,
And that the hated creature wants to keep
You here in the dark to be his lover?
In case that's true, I will stay with you
And never from this dark place
Will I depart. Here, here I will stay
With the worms that surround you. Here
I will stay forever
And shake off all the hardship that fate has dealt me
From my weary body. Eyes, look at her for the last time!
Arms, hug her for the last time! And, lips, that
Allow me to breathe, close forever after one last kiss.
A fair deal for death which is inescapable!

Come, bitter conduct, come, unsavoury guide!
Thou desperate pilot, now at once run on
The dashing rocks thy seasick weary bark!
Here's to my love!

Drinks

O true apothecary!
Thy drugs are quick. Thus with a kiss I die.

Dies

Enter, at the other end of the churchyard, FRIAR LAWRENCE, with a lantern, crow, and spade

FRIAR LAWRENCE
Saint Francis be my speed! how oft to-night
Have my old feet stumbled at graves! Who's there?

BALTHASAR
Here's one, a friend, and one that knows you well.

FRIAR LAWRENCE
Bliss be upon you! Tell me, good my friend,
What torch is yond that vainly lends his light
To grubs and eyeless skulls? As I discern,
It burneth in the Capels' monument.

BALTHASAR
It doth so, holy sir, and there's my master,
One that you love.

FRIAR LAWRENCE
Who is it?

BALTHASAR
Romeo.

FRIAR LAWRENCE
How long hath he been there?

BALTHASAR
Full half an hour.

Now for the next step - the unpleasant bit!
The extreme act that will immediately
Take all the life from my body!
Here's to Juliet!

Drinks

Oh, Mr Chemist!
Your poison works quick. And so with a kiss I die.

Dies

Enter, at the other end of the churchyard, FRIAR LAWRENCE, with a lantern, crow, and spade

FRIAR LAWRENCE
God help me! So many times tonight
I've tripped over graves! Who's that?

BALTHASAR
A friend - someone that knows you well.

FRIAR LAWRENCE
God bless you! Tell me, friend,
What is that light which is shining pointlessly
In this place of worms and bones? As far as I can tell,
It's in the Capulet tomb.

BALTHASAR
It is, Friar. And that's where my master is.
Someone you know well.

FRIAR LAWRENCE
Who is it?

BALTHASAR
Romeo.

FRIAR LAWRENCE
How long has he been here?

BALTHASAR
Half an hour.

FRIAR LAWRENCE
Go with me to the vault.

BALTHASAR
I dare not, sir
My master knows not but I am gone hence,
And fearfully did menace me with death,
If I did stay to look on his intents.

FRIAR LAWRENCE
Stay then, I'll go alone. Fear comes upon me.
O, much I fear some ill unthrifty thing.

BALTHASAR
As I did sleep under this yew-tree here,
I dreamt my master and another fought,
And that my master slew him.

FRIAR LAWRENCE
Romeo!

Advances

Alack, alack, what blood is this which stains
The stony entrance of this sepulchre?
What mean these masterless and gory swords
To lie discoloured by this place of peace?

Enters the tomb

Romeo! O, pale! Who else? What, Paris too?
And steeped in blood? Ah, what an unkind hour
Is guilty of this lamentable chance!
The lady stirs.

JULIET wakes

JULIET
O comfortable Friar, where is my lord?
I do remember well where I should be;
And there I am. Where is my Romeo?

Noise within

FRIAR LAWRENCE
Come with me to the tomb.

BALTHASAR
I daren't, sir.
Romeo thinks I've already left
And he threatened to kill me
If I stayed to spy on him.

FRIAR LAWRENCE
Wait here, then. I'll go on my own. I suddenly feel scared.
I fear something terrible has happened.

BALTHASAR
While I was asleep under this yew tree here,
I dreamt that Romeo fought with another man
And that Romeo killed him.

FRIAR LAWRENCE
Romeo!

Advances

Oh no, oh no, whose blood is this that covers
The stones at the entrance of the tomb?
What are these abandoned blood-stained swords
Doing in this usually peaceful place?

Enters the tomb

Romeo! Oh, no! What else? What? Paris?
And covered in blood? Oh, what a terrible time
Full of terrible things!
Juliet's waking up.

JULIET wakes

JULIET
Friar Lawrence! Where is Romeo?
I remember where I was supposed to be.
And so I am. Where is Romeo?

Noise within

FRIAR LAWRENCE
I hear some noise, lady. Come from that nest
Of death, contagion, and unnatural sleep.
A greater power than we can contradict
Hath thwarted our intents. Come, come away.
Thy husband in thy bosom there lies dead;
And Paris too. Come, I'll dispose of thee
Among a sisterhood of holy nuns.
Stay not to question, for the Watch is coming.
Come, go, good Juliet,

Noise again

I dare no longer stay.

JULIET
Go get thee hence, for I will not away.

Exit FRIAR LAWRENCE

What's here? a cup closed in my true love's hand?
Poison I see hath been his timeless end:
O churl, drunk all, and left no friendly drop
To help me after? I will kiss thy lips,
Haply some poison yet doth hang on them,
To make die with a restorative.

Kisses him

Thy lips are warm.

First Watchman
[Within] Lead, boy, which way?

JULIET
Yea, noise? Then I'll be brief. O happy dagger,

Snatching ROMEO's dagger

This is thy sheath;

Stabs herself

FRIAR LAWRENCE
I hear something. Juliet, come away from this place
Of death, disease, and everlasting sleep.
A greater set of circumstances than we could predict
Has ruined our plans. Come on. Come with me.
Your husband lies dead beside you there.
And Paris is dead too. Come on, I'll take you to
A convent of nuns.
Don't wait to ask questions, the guards are coming.
Come on, let's go. Please, Juliet.

Noise again

We can't wait any longer.

JULIET
Go on then, go. I'm not going anywhere.

Exit FRIAR LAWRENCE

What's this thing clenched in Romeo's hand?
I see poison has been the cause of his death
Oh, shame! You've drunk all of it and not left any
For me so I can do the same. I will kiss your lips -
Hopefully some poison will still be on them
So I can die from the same thing and be reunited.

Kisses him

Your lips are warm.

First Watchman
[Within] Go on, boy. Which way?

JULIET
Someone's coming? Then I'll be quick. This dagger

Snatching ROMEO's dagger

Will go here.

Stabs herself

there rust, and let me die.

Falls on ROMEO's body, and dies

Enter Watch, with the Page of PARIS

PAGE
This is the place, there where the torch doth burn.

First Watchman
The ground is bloody, search about the churchyard.
Go, some of you, whoe'er you find attach.
Pitiful sight! here lies the County slain,
And Juliet bleeding, warm, and newly dead,
Who here hath lain these two days buriéd.
Go tell the Prince, run to the Capulets,
Raise up the Montagues; some others search.
We see the ground whereon these woes do lie,
But the true ground of all these piteous woes
We cannot without circumstance descry.

Re-enter some of the Watch, with BALTHASAR

Second Watchman
Here's Romeo's man, we found him in the churchyard.

First Watchman
Hold him in safety till the Prince come hither.

Re-enter others of the Watch, with FRIAR LAWRENCE

Third Watchman
Here is a friar that trembles, sighs and weeps:
We took this mattock and this spade from him,
As he was coming from this churchyard's side.

First Watchman
A great suspicion. Stay the Friar too.

Enter the PRINCE and Attendants

PRINCE
What misadventure is so early up,
That calls our person from our morning's rest?

Let it stay there forever so I can die.

Falls on ROMEO's body, and dies

Enter Watch, with the Page of PARIS

PAGE
This is the place where the torch was burning.

First Watchman
The ground is covered in blood. Search the churchyard.
Go on, you lot. Arrest whoever you find.
Oh, what a terrible sight! The Count has been killed,
And Juliet is bleeding, warm, and only newly dead.
Yet she was buried two days ago.
Go, tell the Prince. Someone go to the Capulets.
Get the Montagues. The rest of you search.
We can see where these terrible things have happened
But the reason for these awful events
We can't currently work out.

Re-enter some of the Watch, with BALTHASAR

Second Watchman
Here's Romeo's servant. We found him in the churchyard.

First Watchman
Hold on to him until the Prince arrives.

Re-enter others of the Watch, with FRIAR LAWRENCE

Third Watchman
Here is a Friar – he's shaking, sighing and weeping.
We took this pickaxe and this spade from him.
He was heading from this side of the churchyard.

First Watchman
Very suspicious. Hold on to him too.

Enter the PRINCE and Attendants

PRINCE
What has happened so early in the morning
That means I have to be woken up?

Enter CAPULET, LADY CAPULET, and others

CAPULET
What should it be, that is so shrieked abroad?

LADY CAPULET
O, the people in the street cry 'Romeo',
Some 'Juliet', and some 'Paris', and all run
With open outcry toward our monument.

PRINCE
What fear is this which startles in our ears?

First Watchman
Sovereign, here lies the County Paris slain,
And Romeo dead, and Juliet, dead before,
Warm and new killed.

PRINCE
Search, seek, and know how this foul murder comes.

First Watchman
Here is a friar, and slaughtered Romeo's man,
With instruments upon them, fit to open
These dead men's tombs.

CAPULET
O heavens! O wife, look how our daughter bleeds!
This dagger hath mistane, for lo, his house
Is empty on the back of Montague,
And it mis-sheathed in my daughter's bosom!

LADY CAPULET
O me, this sight of death is as a bell,
That warns my old age to a sepulchre.

Enter MONTAGUE and others

PRINCE
Come, Montague, for thou art early up,
To see thy son and heir more early down.

Enter CAPULET, LADY CAPULET, and others

CAPULET
What's all this that people are shouting about?

LADY CAPULET
People in the street are saying 'Romeo',
Some say 'Juliet' and some say 'Paris' and all are running,
Crying, towards our tomb.

PRINCE
What terrible thing could have caused all this?

First Watchman
Prince, Count Paris lies here killed.
And Romeo is dead. And Juliet, who was already dead,
Is warm and only recently killed.

PRINCE
Investigate and find out how this happened.

First Watchman
Here is a Friar and Romeo's servant
With tools on them which could be used to open
The tomb.

CAPULET
Oh, God! Wife, look - our daughter is bleeding!
This dagger's in the wrong place - it should be used
On a Montague
And instead it's here in my daughter's chest!

LADY CAPULET
Oh no! This terrible sight is as an omen
That leads me closer to my own death.

Enter MONTAGUE and others

PRINCE
Come here, Montague. You're up early
To see your son and heir laid low.

MONTAGUE
Alas, my liege, my wife is dead tonight;
Grief of my son's exile hath stopped her breath:
What further woe conspires against mine age?

PRINCE
Look and thou shalt see.

MONTAGUE
O thou untaught! what manners is in this,
To press before thy father to a grave?

PRINCE
Seal up the mouth of outrage for a while,
Till we can clear these ambiguities,
And know their spring, their head, their
true descent,
And then will I be general of your woes,
And lead you even to death. Mean time forbear,
And let mischance be slave to patience.
Bring forth the parties of suspicion.

FRIAR LAWRENCE
I am the greatest, able to do least,
Yet most suspected, as the time and place
Doth make against me, of this direful murder;
And here I stand, both to impeach and purge
Myself condemnéd and myself excused.

PRINCE
Then say at once what thou dost know in this.

FRIAR LAWRENCE
I will be brief, for my short date of breath
Is not so long as is a tedious tale.
Romeo, there dead, was husband to that Juliet,
And she, there dead, that Romeo's faithful wife:
I married them, and their stol'n marriage day
Was Tybalt's doomsday, whose untimely death
Banished the new-made bridegroom from the city,
For whom, and not for Tybalt, Juliet pined.
You, to remove that siege of grief from her,
Betrothed and would have married her perforce
To County Paris. Then comes she to me,
And, with wild looks, bid me devise some mean
To rid her from this second marriage,

MONTAGUE
Sadly, Prince, my wife died tonight.
The grief of my son's banishment caused her death.
What more misery must I face in my old age?

PRINCE
Look and you'll see.

MONTAGUE
Oh, please, no! How can it be
That my son has died before me?

PRINCE
Don't say anything more for the moment
Until we can work out what this is all about
And know what caused it, how it started, and what happened.
And then I will comfort you in your sadness
And help you for as long as I live. For now, wait -
Hold off from your sorrow for a little while longer.
Bring forward the suspects.

FRIAR LAWRENCE
I am the greatest in status and, though the least dangerous,
Am suspected the most as the time and place
Cause people suspect me of this terrible murder.
I am here both to accuse and pardon -
To condemn myself and exonerate myself.

PRINCE
Then tell me right now what you know about this.

FRIAR LAWRENCE
I will be quick because what I have to say
Is not a long and boring story.
Romeo, who lies there dead, was married to Juliet.
And she, who is also dead, was Romeo's wife.
I married them and their secret wedding day
Was the same day Tybalt died - whose unfortunate death
Caused the bridegroom to be banished from the city.
It was for him, and not for Tybalt, that Juliet pined.
You, to help her overcome her grief,
Arranged her marriage and would have wed her by force
To Count Paris so she came to me
And, in desperation, asked me to think of some way
To get out of this second marriage

Or in my cell there would she kill herself.
Then gave I her, so tutored by my art,
A sleeping potion, which so took effect
As I intended, for it wrought on her
The form of death. Mean time I writ to Romeo,
That he should hither come as this dire night
To help to take her from her borrowed grave,
Being the time the potion's force should cease.
But he which bore my letter, Friar John,
Was stayed by accident, and yesternight
Returned my letter back. Then all alone
At the prefixed hour of her waking,
Came I to take her from her kindred's vault;
Meaning to keep her closely at my cell,
Till I conveniently could send to Romeo.
But when I came, some minute ere the time
Of her awakening, here untimely lay
The noble Paris and true Romeo dead.
She wakes, and I entreated her come forth
And bear this work of heaven with patience.
But then a noise did scare me from the tomb,
And she too desperate would not go with me,
But as it seems, did violence on herself.
All this I know, and to the marriage
Her nurse is privy; and if ought in this
Miscarried by my fault, let my old life
Be sacrificed, some hour before his time,
Unto the rigour of severest law.

PRINCE
We still have known thee for a holy man.
Where's Romeo's man? what can he say in this?

BALTHASAR
I brought my master news of Juliet's death,
And then in post he came from Mantua
To this same place, to this same monument.
This letter he early bid me give his father,
And threatened me with death, going in the vault,
I departed not and left him there.

PRINCE
Give me the letter, I will look on it.
Where is the County's page, that raised the Watch?
Sirrah, what made your master in this place?

Or, in my church, she would kill herself.
So I gave her, as I had learnt to make,
A sleeping potion which worked
As I intended for it made her
Look dead. In the meantime I wrote to Romeo
That he should come here tonight
To help to rescue her from her temporary *grave*
At the time the potion was due to wear off.
But the man who took my letter, Friar John,
Was unfortunately delayed and yesterday
Brought my letter back to me. Then, on my own,
At the time it was planned she would wake up,
I came to take her from her family tomb -
Intending to keep her hidden at my church
Until I could secretly send a message to Romeo.
But when I arrived, shortly before she was due
To wake up, I found
The bodies of Paris and Romeo.
She woke up and I begged her to come with me
And deal with these events in due time.
Then I heard a noise which made me run from the tomb.
She was determined not to go with me
And instead, it seems, decided to kill herself.
This is all I know. As to the marriage -
Her nurse knew about it. And, if any of this
Went wrong because of me, then may my life
Be taken before my time,
In whatever harsh manner the law allows.

PRINCE
We know you are a holy man.
Where's Romeo's servant? What does he have to say?

BALTHASAR
I brought Romeo news of Juliet's death
And he quickly came here from Mantua
To this exact place, to this exact tomb.
He asked me to give this letter to his father
And threatened to kill me as he entered the tomb
If I didn't go and leave him to it.

PRINCE
Give me the letter - I will look at it.
Where is the Count's servant who fetched the guards?
You - what was your master doing here?

PAGE
He came with flowers to strew his lady's grave,
And bid me stand aloof, and so I did.
Anon comes one with light to ope the tomb,
And by and by my master drew on him,
And then I ran away to call the Watch.

PRINCE
This letter doth make good the Friar's words,
Their course of love, the tidings of her death;
And here he writes that he did buy a poison
Of a poor pothecary, and therewithal
Came to this vault to die, and lie with Juliet.
Where be these enemies? Capulet, Montague?
See what a scourge is laid upon your hate,
That heaven finds means to kill your joys with love!
And I for winking at your discords too
Have lost a brace of kinsmen. All are punished.

CAPULET
O brother Montague, give me thy hand.
This is my daughter's jointure, for no more
Can I demand.

MONTAGUE
But I can give thee more,
For I will raise her statue in pure gold,
That while Verona by that name is known,
There shall no figure at such rate be set
As that of true and faithful Juliet.

CAPULET
As rich shall Romeo's by his lady's lie;
Poor sacrifices of our enmity!

PRINCE
A glooming peace this morning with it brings,
The sun for sorrow will not show his head.
Go hence to have more talk of these sad things;
Some shall be pardoned, and some punishéd:
For never was a story of more woe
Than this of Juliet and her Romeo.

Exeunt

PAGE
He came to put flowers on Juliet's grave
And told me to wait outside - so I did.
Soon after someone came with a light to open the tomb
And not long after that my master drew his sword on him.
That's when I ran to fetch the guards.

PRINCE
This letter proves what the Friar said -
The story of their love, the news of her death.
And here he says that he bought a poison
From a poor chemist and afterwards
Came to this tomb to die and be with Juliet.
Where are the feuding families? Capulet! Montague!
See what a terrible thing has been caused by your fighting
That God has found a way to kill your happiness with love.
And, because I overlooked your feuding, I too
Have lost several friends. We have all been punished.

CAPULET
Montague, give me your hand.
This is my daughter's legacy - no more fighting
I insist.

MONTAGUE
I will go further.
I will make a statue of her out of gold
That, for as long Verona stays standing,
There will not be any statue as fine
As that of your wonderful Juliet.

CAPULET
And I'll do the same for Romeo to stand beside her -
The poor victims of our hatred.

PRINCE
This morning has brought with it a sad peace.
It's so sad that even the sun won't show itself.
You can go now and talk more about these sad events.
Some will find solace, and some further torment.
Because there was never a story as tragic
As that of Romeo and Juliet.

Exeunt

ABOUT THE AUTHOR

Gabrielle Winters was born and raised in the Home Counties. She holds a BSc (Hons) in Psychology and devotes her time to supporting various charitable causes including The Rose Playhouse in Southwark.

Printed in Great Britain
by Amazon